CW00336633

NEW RETRO

GRAPHICS & LOGOS IN RETRO STYLE

FIRST PUBLISHED AND DISTIBUTED BY
VICTION:WORKSHOP LTD.

viction:ary™

VICTION:WORKSHOP LTD.
UNIT C, 7/F, SEABRIGHT PLAZA, 9-23 SHELL STREET,
NORTH POINT, HONG KONG
URL: VICTIONARY.COM   EMAIL: WE@VICTIONARY.COM

🅕 @VICTIONWORKSHOP
🅞 @VICTIONWORKSHOP
Bē @VICTIONARY
🅟 @VICTIONARY

EDITED AND PRODUCED BY VICTION:ARY
CONCEPTS & ART DIRECTION BY VICTOR CHEUNG
BOOK DESIGN BY VICTION:WORKSHOP LTD.

©2021 VICTION:WORKSHOP LTD.
ALL RIGHTS RESERVED. NO PART OF THIS PUBLICATION MAY BE
REPRODUCED, STORED IN RETRIEVAL SYSTEMS OR TRANSMITTED IN ANY
FORM OR BY ANY MEANS, ELECTRONIC, MECHANICAL, PHOTOCOPYING,
RECORDING OR ANY INFORMATION STORAGE, WITHOUT WRITTEN
PERMISSIONS FROM RESPECTIVE COPYRIGHT OWNER(S).

COPYRIGHT ON TEXT AND DESIGN WORK IS HELD BY RESPECTIVE
DESIGNERS AND CONTRIBUTORS. ALL ARTWORK AND TEXTUAL INFORMATION
IN THIS BOOK ARE BASED ON THE MATERIALS OFFERED BY DESIGNERS
WHOSE WORK HAS BEEN INCLUDED. WHILE EVERY EFFORT HAS BEEN MADE
TO ENSURE THEIR ACCURACY, VICTION:WORKSHOP DOES NOT ACCEPT
ANY RESPONSIBILITY, UNDER ANY CIRCUMSTANCES, FOR ANY ERRORS OR
OMISSIONS.

ISBN 978-988-74629-4-1
PRINTED AND BOUND IN CHINA

GRAPHICS & LOGOS

NEW RETRO IS A GRAPHIC NOD
TO THE AESTHETICS AND VALUES THAT
WITHSTAND TIME.

NEW RETRO

G R A P H I C S

L O G O S

MADE IN

RETRO STYLE

Limited Release

NEW RETRO FEATURES IDENTITIES, VISUAL
COMMUNICATIONS, PACKAGING, EDITORIAL AND
INTERIOR DESIGN.

20TH ANNIVERSARY EDITION

CORPORATE IDENTITY

SELECTED WORKS

ESTᴰ ✕ ⇥ DESIGNED & *Victionary* PUBLISHED ⇤ ✕ 2021

HAND DRAWING

SELECTED WORKS

At a time when the graphic design industry has to deal with a big economic change, our work confronted the change with a contemporary graphic approach using traditional printing techniques that may be considered ancestral for some. We love to keep our hands on a good book or touch a beautiful poster to perceive the subtlety of its print or frame, feel the relief of ink under our fingers and assume that the overprints are there to contribute memorable experiences. We love working with craftsmen who have knowledge and skills in traditional techniques. The sharing and exchange of ideas are very beneficial for the successful completion of our projects.

The "NEW RETRO" emerges when two epochs meet. Our duo devotion to fine prints and creative experiments are combined with the practical knowledge of an able craftsman. By uniting traditional production techniques and mediums with contemporary graphic design, our approach highlights the attractive qualities of printed matter and creates a dialogue in a play on both visual impact and touch.

During the creative process, we devote a lot of time to research paper, printing process and matching colour schemes. A good design may become even better during this set of steps. Sometimes the printing process comes right at the start of our design conception, deriving a design based largely on the technique.

When it comes to our graphic style, our approach is largely drawn on Swiss reductive philosophies, such as Modernism and International Typographic Style. While designers from these movements advocated an accurate focus on the basics without frills for visual efficiency, we also try to bring our own interpretation and global influences our times provide us into our design — influences that naturally come from the multitude of images in the media, internet, the street and museums. By incorporating these influences into subjects represented by their most significant forms, we embrace the age-old principles into modern vocabularies and produce results that are the cleanest and most powerful and relevant to the users ever.

Our interest in combining techniques has been very present across our work, from how we create graphics out of digitalised linocut patterns to the production of our silkscreen posters. When a balanced design is achieved, there's where the peak of perfection lies — when graphics guided with programmed rules is matched with imperfection brought about by an old typographic machine.

THE "NEW RETRO" EMERGES WHEN OUR DUO DEVOTION TO FINE PRINTS AND CREATIVE EXPERIMENTS ARE COMBINED WITH THE PRACTICAL KNOWLEDGE OF AN ABLE CRAFTSMAN.

— A3 Studio —

THE KNOWLEDGE OF THE VISUAL FORM OF RETRO ELEMENTS AND ITS HISTORY, TOGETHER WITH THE UNDERSTANDING OF THE CONTEXT OF THE PROJECT ARE TWO VITAL PARTS OF THE EQUATION.

– Foreign Policy Design Group –

Retro:. /'retrō/. Adjective

Imitative of a style, fashion, or design from the recent past.*

The etymology of the word retro is the abbreviation of rétrograde 'retrograde'. Retrograde means going back in time or position.

Design, art, film, theatre, story telling – all forms of creative endeavours entail the process of inspiration, invention and creation. As creatives, we are wired to instinctually and quickly get our hands and brains around anything we find inspiring or suitable for the context of what we are designing for. We research, learn, and then perhaps tweak or simplify or deconstruct or simply re-apply the style wholesale to our work. Sometimes we just collect, archive and hoard any kind of materials we come across like what geeks do and wait to use them one day. (The truth, and you know it, is actually we cannot wait to use them in a project right away!) Such sources of inspiration many times come from elements or style from the past. Human beings are basically a pretty sentimental lot – we have an innate tendency to like that fuzzy warm nostalgic experience, whether we ourselves had actually lived through it or not. We are inclined to enjoy recalling and fitting those experiences into our current ones. We, creatives, love to jolt these memories and evoke these emotions; we like to re-create that moment and re-apply or adapt it to our modern culture and contemporary lifestyle. We believe that our audience will respond to that and enjoy that moment as well.

When we were working on the branding for restaurant HayMarket in Hong Kong, the city being an ex-British colony immediately came to us as something we could hark back to using colonial era graphics. The Hong Kong Jockey Club, the historic colonial building where HayMarket is nestled, gave us further nostalgic elements to play and layer with. We were inspired by the colours and patterns from jockey silks, vintage British typography and Victorian-style illustrations from old advertisements. These ingredients came together perfectly as a great cocktail of quirky and eccentric British traits that aptly suited HayMarket's brand.

It is necessary to apply retro or vintage visuals with care especially these elements are associated to a certain story and experience in time. It is therefore critical to get a crisp understanding of these historical background before any sort of application. The results would be very neat if executed appropriately to the context and concept. However, sometimes we do have to re-adjust the visual language to befit our storyline so that it connects to the current culture for the audience to be more emotionally attached to the brand.

The same applies to the choice of typefaces. Just like Blackletters, also sometimes known as Gothic, Fraktur or Old English, which is a script used throughout Western Europe from circa 1150 through to the 17th century, characterised by its dramatic thin and thick strokes and sometimes the elaborate swirls on the serifs, created based on early manuscript lettering. Blackletter was used in one of the first printed books, Gutenburg Bible, written in Latin and massively reproduced with movable types. But they can become extremely difficult to read as a body text throughout an entire page. An actual example that appeared in the menu of a medieval-style restaurant in Bratislava, Slovakia, when Blackletter was used for the description for each menu item, set in four different languages with diacritics in the Slavic languages. This meant the reader has to seek out for his/her language amongst the stacks. However it will be a totally different picture if the designer of the menu had considered using the Blackletter simply as a header and sub-headers while adopting a more legible font for the food description, a font that is complementary to Blackletter. That way this will aid legibility while still being capable of retaining that medieval feel.

In essence, the knowledge of the visual form of retro elements and its history, together with the understanding of the context of the project are two vital parts of the equation when concocting that cocktail using vintage elements as an ingredient – the appropriateness lies in the hands of the designer.

* "Retro" Def. 1. *Oxford American Dictionary*, Oxford University Press, n.d. Web. 25 Jan. 2016.

★ RETRO ★
IN
ICONS

BE IT TYPOGRAPHY-BASED DESIGN OR PURE GRAPHICS, THESE LOGOTYPES AND EMBLEMS EPITOMISE HOW AGE-OLD AESTHETICS ADD VALUE TO MODERN DESIGN IN SMALL DIMENSIONS. GROUPED NEATLY BY THE NAMES OF RESPECTIVE DESIGNERS, AND ARRANGED BY FORM AND STYLE, THIS EYE-CATCHING COLLECTION OF LOGO MARKS SHOWCASES THE DIVERSE EMBODIMENT OF VINTAGE LETTERFORMS, GRAPHICS AND ICONOGRAPHY THAT SOLIDIFY THE CONNECTION OF A BRAND WITH THE GLAMOROUS PAST. A UNIFIED MONOCHROMATIC SHOWCASE ACCENTUATES THE INTRICATE STRUCTURE AND GRAPHICAL DETAILS OF THESE MINIATURE DESIGNS.

P. 010 —————— P. 095

1

2

3

4

5

6

7

1.Austin & Austin Café, Bar & Lounge 2.Genuine Articles 3.Leonart Motorcycles 4.Motos Hernández
5.Trackswear Vinyl & Wood Sunglasses 6.Ristorante Pizza di Piero 7.The Cigar Company

Adam Ewing Advertising & Editorial Photography

1

2

3

4

5

6

7

8

1.Ars Magna Antiques 2.Astoon Tattoo Studio 3.Moto Kickstart 4.Iron & Air Magazine 5.Joel Gott Wines
6.Crd Café Racer Dreams 7.Ristorante Piazze d'Italia 8.La Gran Tasca Restaurant & Bar

1

2

3

4

5

1.Monegros Cycles 2.Fox Racing 3.Adam Ewing Advertising & Editorial Photography
4.Oily Rag Clothing Co. 5.Tazza d'Oro National Barista Championship

Motos Hernández

1

2

1.Pure&Crafted Festival
2.Gascap Motors

Gascap Motors

Gascap Motors

1

2

1.Gascap Motors
2.Oily Rag Clothing Co.

1.The Three Thieves Winery 2.Monegros Cycles
3.Crd Cream Motorcycles 4.Harley-Davidson Motorcycles

1.Seventy Eight Motor Co.
2.Crd Café Racer Dreams

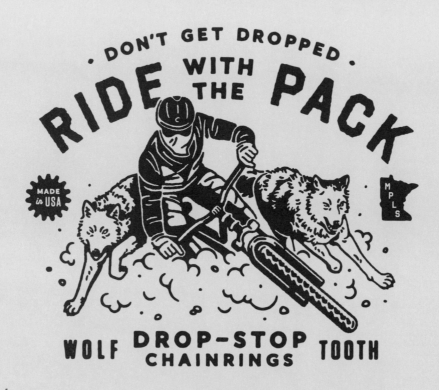

1

2

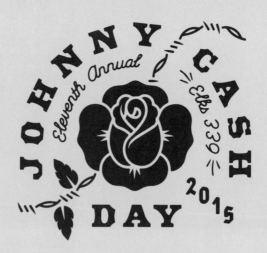

3

1.Wolf Tooth - Ride With the Pack by Alana Louise
2.Bayardstown Big Bottle by Colin Miller 3.Johnny Cash Day 2015 by Colin Miller

1. SPEAK SOFT & WORK HARD · THE HUMBLE · CO · BARBER · H B

2. THE Proper KNOT

THE Proper Knot

3. UP LATE · Studio A.M. · UP EARLY

4. Made IN PGH

5. Look Up More

6.

NEVER MEND YOU — OR TAILOR MORE

1.Humble Hand 2.Proper Knot 3.Studio A.M.
4.Made in Pittsburgh 5.Look Up More 6.This Is A Fire Door

OWN *TO* TRADE

MOTO
ROSTER

TRADE *TO* OWN

1

2   3   4

1.Moto Roster 2.Hop Star 3.Look Up More 4.Northeastish

1

2

ROCKETFIT
FIELD DIVISION
ATLANTA, GA.
U.S.A

ROCKETFIT
ATLANTA
GA. U.S.A
FIELD DIVISION

3

4

5

6

1.Remember Superica 2.Superica Kitchen Tee 3.RocketFit Field Division
4.Commonplace Pocketknife 5.The Good Folks Co. Square Knot 6.RocketFit Squad

-025-

1

2

3

4

5

6

7

8

1.Corner Market 2.Tamarack Homes 3.Oxford House Bed and Breakfast 4.Quilchena Cattle Company
5.Lehome Vintage Furniture 6.Atomic Coffee Roasters 7.Black Hole Beer Company 8.Rocket Slide Films

1

2

3

4

5

6

7

8

1.Hewsons Hardware 2.Deuce Cafe 3.Jalopy Journal 4.Jukebox Print
5.Rays Lawn Care 6.Jakes Homestyle Restaurant 7.Johnny's Speed Shop 8.Danny Boy Beer Works

1

2

3

4

5

6

7

8

1.Crisp & Co. 2.Early Bird Espresso & Brew Bar 3.Waterways French Bistro 4.Tazito World Burrito
5.Detroit Ham & Corned Beef Co. 6.Glades Brewing Co. 7.Cotton Company 8.BYDFAULT

1

2

3

4

5

6

7

1.Red Hill Collision Repair 2.Art Bergmann 3.Iron & Air Magazine 4.Red Bomber Productions
5.Side Car Coffee Roasters 6.Vinnie's Restaurant 7.Highflyers Public House

1

2

1.1950s Storefront logos
2.Deco Dolls Make-up and Hairstyling

1

2

1.Gordano Home Front 2.Travel labels

TRADICIÓN   FAMILIAR

Cecilia de Quiroz

MEZCAL

1

O Y S T E R S & C O

BAR/ BEER AND GRILL

2

1

2

3

4

5

1.PIG´S PEARLS 2.Dionnysius 3.ROMEA
4.RIVADAVIA 5.Ofelia Villáseñor

STOLTHED

— ROYAL —

(1988)

1

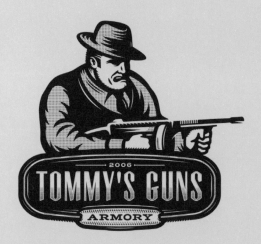

KHAN
THE CONQUEROR

2

3

1.Stolthed Royal 2.Tommy's Guns 3.Khan - The Conqueror

LOUCOMOTION
IMAGERY LAB & APPS FACTORY
Since 2014

1

EMPEROR'S BREWING
Handcrafted Ales and Lagers
—— BREWED IN BELGIUM ——

EMPEROR'S BREWING
Handcrafted Ales and Lagers
—— BREWED IN BELGIUM ——

2

1.Loucomotion Imagery Lab & Apps Factory
2.Emperor's Brewing - Handcrafted Ales and Lagers

1

2

3

4

1.Ponoi River Co. 2.Chickadee Sweets
3.Mill City Fineries Handmade Bow Ties 4.Catalina Candles

1

2

1

2

3

4

1.The Captain's Daughter 2.Caravel Brewing Company
3.Nakua Coffee 4.McArthur Ranch

1

2

3

4

1.Emmu Bottom Homestead - Anzac Biscuits 2.Mad Sons Pub
3.1776 Effects 4.Muzzle Loaders

Marks & badges

DON'T COUNT THE **DAYS** MAKE THE DAYS COUNT

Comparison IS THE THIEF OF JOY

GREATNESS HAS TO BE Earned

YOU ARE Capable OF ANYTHING

Hustle HARDER

TO WIN YOU HAVE TO Risk LOSS

YOU **WIN** SOME ≈ YOU LOSE SOME ═ IT'S ALL ═ PART OF THE Game CALLED LIFE

WE MUSN'T Dwell ON THE NEGATIVE

TRY TO Encourage YOURSELF & OTHERS

Motivational quotes

1

2

3

4

5

6

1.Double Dutch Farms 2.Grit & Thistle Film Company 3.Wild Woods Brewery
4.Guadalupe Brewing Co. 5.SubCulture Cyclery 6.Vino Salida

1

2

3

4

5

6

7

1.Drink Local 2.Colorado Boy Pub & Brewery 3.River's Edge Brewing Co.
4.Caveman Brewing Co. 5.Fate Brewing Co. 6.Elevation Beer Company® 7.Colorado Sky Brewing Co.

1

2

3

4

5

1.Big Beach Brewing Co. 2.Seasons Café 3.Obscure Brewing Co.
4.March Hare Brewing Co. 5.Becky Hersch Hair Studio

1

2

3

1.Montanya Distillers 2.Scottsdale Brewery
3.Salida Guitar Expo

1

2

3

4

1.Young Life 2.Yolo apparel graphics
3.Salida Hydroponic Supply 4.Wanderlust Festival

2

1

3

1.Colorado Brewers Rendezvous
2.Smile Kite School 3.Sunday Lounge

1

2

1.Barnett & Son Brewing Co. 2.Guidestone Colorado

1

2

3

1.Blindsight Brewing 2.Becky Hersch Hair Studio
3.Vault Brewing Company

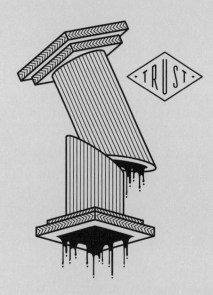

Trust the Buzz

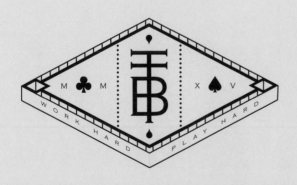

Trust the Buzz

American Vintage Badges Part Two

American Vintage Badges Part Three

American Vintage Badges Part Four

THE LUMBERJACK CO

Blue RIDGE · North CAROLINA 1969

MOUNTAINS

A LIFE AMONG THE EVERGREENS

WILD TERRITORY *The* STRONG BEARS ©

MOUNTAINS

GREY WOLF HUNTER

OUTDOOR -THE- LONELY WOLF BROSS

ADVENTURE MISSISSIPI - STORE -

IN A WORLD THAT'S CHANGING I'M A *Stranger* IN A STRANGE LAND

WHO AM I *to* DECIDE

WHAT SHOULD BE DONE

YELLOWSTONE PARK

THE HOUSE OF THE *American Buffalo* CO.

IDAHO MONTANA WYOMING

THE TRAVELERS DUCKS

NORTH *to* SOUTH · SOUTH *to* NORTH CO.

1975

ESTB · SEARCHING · BROS

A NEW DESTINY

STRONG IN THIS
-LIFE-
Fighting Grizzly
FREE FOREVER

UNTIL THE END

HALCON
FREE
Co.
75

- UNTIL THE END -

-HEAR THE TREES-
LUMBERJACK
Co.
19   75

WORKER OF THIS LAND

— IN THE —
DESERT
OF *Life*

I FIND MYSELF
- ARIZONA -

-THE BRAVE NATIVE-
— *The* —
AMERICAN
75   Co.

BISON
OWNER OF THIS LAND

1

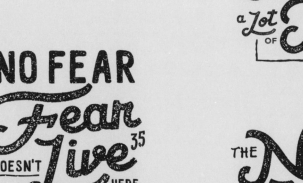

2

1.Americano typeface 2.American Forkball typeface

"THEY DON'T WANT THE CLASSIC HORROR FILMS ANYMORE."

Bela Lugosi ™
(1882-1956)

Bela Lugosi

· SLOW FOOD FAST ·

1

WOLFFE

◄ INDUSTRIES ►

FORM & FUNCTION

2

Seven Days a Week Print Shoppe

Seven Days a Week Print Shoppe

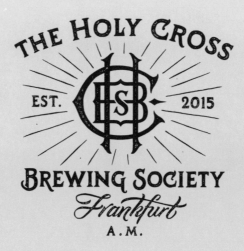

The Holy Cross Brewing Society

1

2

3

4

1.The Studio at Climber's Rock 2.Stoff aus Frankfurt
3.Wasted Steel on Wheels 4.Seven Days a Week Print Shoppe

GRAPHIC DESIGN
CALIFORNIA
STEVEN
freelancer

Exclusive Shop
STREET
EST. **NEW YORK** 2020
PREMIUM STYLE
MADE IN UNITED STATES

RETRO VINTAGE STYLE
blacksuit
CLOTHING
INTERNATIONAL BRAND

THE COFFEE SHOP
The Retro
RESTAURANT
New York

BEST FOOD AND BEER
SINCE 2020
Grill Bill
HAVE FUN AND EAT
TEXAS

FREELANCER
David Roth
PREMIUM STYLE
MADE IN UNITED STATES

New York
LAURA DEFELICE
FASHION DESIGNER
a way of living

BLUE SKY
DAVID PETTERSON
AWESOME STYLE
Vip Only

Vintage logos & labels

CHANDLER

PHOTOGRAPHY

EST. 2020

Photography

JESSICA

ANDERSON

EST. 2020

VINTAGE STYLE

EST. 2020

YARD

exclusive

NEW YORK

Designer

GEORGE

— LUXURY —

new york

Vip Only

KINGSTONE

BEER AND DRINKS

THE PREMIUM STYLE

THE COFFEE SHOP

MICHAEL JONES

RESTAURANT

london

EST. 2020

RESTAURANT

Don Julio

BEER AND DRINKS

PREMIUM

Los Angeles

EST. **MONTES** 2020

LUXURY CLOTHING

modern design

THE EXCLUSIVE PROJECT

RETRO GROUP

UNITED STATES PROJECT

FUTURE BRAND

RETRO HOUSE

Vintage

EST. 2020

THE HOUSE OF YOUR DREAMS

EST. 1984

THE MARKET

VINTAGE

NEW YORK

THE VINTAGE APPLE

RESTAURANT

THE AMERICAN BADGE

Exclusive

EST. 2020

CLEVELANT

VINTAGE

CLOTHING

EST. 2020

MEAT AND BEER

Collection

HALFSIDE

CLOTHING

EST. 2020

THE CASTLE

EST. 1984

RETRO STYLE

Vintage logos & labels

Vintage logos & labels

Vintage logos & labels

1.Monster Children Magazine 2.Dashing & Co. 3.Local Wolves Wine
4.The Sheepdogs 5.Pemberton Music Festival 6.Phish Fall Tour 2014

1

2

3

4

5

6

1.Newport Folk Festival 2.Morphē Jewelry 3.Phish Summer Tour 2015
4.The Hand & Eye 5.Black Wolf Press 6.Mumford & Sons

1

2

3

4

5

1.WRKSHOP 2.Essence Music 3.RAM Customs
4.Audax Suisse Cycling 5.The Frame Theory

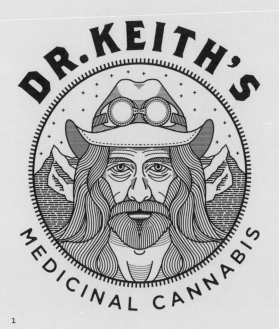

1

2

3

4

1.Dr. Keith's Medicinal Cannabis 2.The Good Doctor
3.The Decemberists 4.Josh Ritter

1

2

3

4

1.Crow Thief 2.Sad Cat Blues Bar 3.Indian Gardens
4.Ruthsteam Adventure Buddies

1

2

3

4

5

6

1.Owl & Lark Coffee & Juice Bar 2.Adam Snow 3.Arawak Cycles
4.Roupala 5.Sly Loris Hot Sauce 6.Brian Steely personal branding

1

2

3

4

5

6

7

8

1.Nash Garage 2.Not All Who Wander Want to be Found 3.Hobo and Sailor 4.The Bean Shop
5.Coffee Bob Cafe 6.Jim Aero 7.Black Fox Press 8.Bonaci Seafood

Scandinavia Club

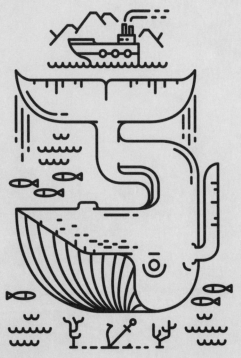

Scandinavia Club

ISADORA

LO PRECIOSO // DE LO VIL

ABCDEFG
HIJKLMNN
OPQRSTU
VWXYZ&
1234567890

Clásica, humanista...

orgánica, limpia

Isadora Calligraphy typeface

Isadora Calligraphy typeface

CALIFORNIA

CALLIGRAPHIC FONT

si sacaréis lo precioso de lo vil...

Isadora Calligraphy typeface

CALLIGRAPHIC FONT

lo precioso de lo vil...

Isadora Calligraphy typeface

1

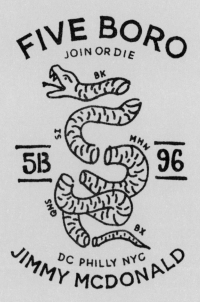

2

3

1.5Boro Cinco Barrios II 2.5Boro Don't Tread
3.5Boro Jimmy McDonald City Hall Pro

1

2

1.5050 Skatepark aloha t-shirt 2.Field guide type

American traditional tattoo flash — blue print

American traditional tattoo flash - letterpress

1

2

1.Random logos 2.Nuklheads New York

1

2

3

4

1.International Children's Games 2.Walk in Tainan
3.Good Days in Kyoto 4.Good Walk from Tainan to Kyoto

THE
ANOMALOUS

RARE OCCURANCES

SOULLESS
· CORPSES ·

GODS IN
· MYTHOLOGY ·

EGYPTIAN
· BLACK ·

TALES OF
· FOLKLORE ·

DWELLERS OF
· VIKING'S DEEP ·

TRAILS OF THE
· WOODSMEN ·

MEDIEVAL
THRONES ·

THE KINGDOM OF
· ANCIENT ROME ·

NATIVE
MOTHER ·

1

2

3

4

5

6

1.Goofle 2.Nuevo México 3.Los Pollos Hermanos 4.Marco Gadau
5.Steph Curry 6.Oca Handcraft

ESTᴰ – 013

PETTIROSSO
HANDCRAFT
Gᴇ – IT

1

TX   USA

DIMI ARHONTIDIS
IN
E
S MOTUS 20
T 14
VERITAS
–
STORYTELLING

2

HEY   YOU
–
PROMOTE
GIVE VOICE AT YOUR MESSAGES

3

GAMBERO

4

WEDDING
PORTRAIT

5

The

PENGUIN
SOCIETY

6

BOSCO
dei
CERRI

7

1.Pettirosso Handcraft 2.In Motus Veritas 3.Promote
4.Gambero 5.Darek Novak 6.Penguin Society 7.Bosco dei Cerri

Hiroshima mon amour

Hiroshima mon amour

CD - creative direction
CL - client
CP - copywriting
CR - special credits
DE - design
IL - illustration
IN - interior design
PH - photography
PT - printing

✶ RETRO ✶
IN
DESIGN

THIS CHAPTER IS COMPRISED OF COMPREHENSIVE GRAPHIC
SOLUTIONS GARNERED FROM ESTABLISHED AND EMERGING
DESIGNERS AROUND THE WORLD WHO ALL APPRECIATE
BEAUTY THAT WITHSTANDS TIME. THE SELECTION EXAMINES
HOW TIME-HONOURED VISUAL ELEMENTS SUCH AS PRINT
FINISHES, PATTERNS, ILLUSTRATIONS, PALETTES, AND
CLASSIC TYPEFACES ARE APPLIED TO CREATE FASHIONABLE
IDENTITIES AND COMMUNICATIONS. ACCOMPANYING
DESCRIPTIONS PROVIDE INSIGHT INTO THE DESIGNER'S
INGENUITY OF STRATEGIC BRANDING EVOCATIVE OF
HISTORIC AND CULTURAL CONNOTATIONS.

P. 098 ——————— P. 279

BASIC STAMPS

Duane Dalton

Basic Stamps is an ongoing postage stamp project initiated by Duane Dalton. Marrying his love for design and stamps, the Irish graphic artist has created more than 80 stamp designs with a characteristic approach to turn them into a series. With simple shapes, colours and typefaces, these little art pieces identify a number of countries and organisations with their spirit and landscape.

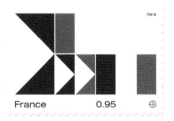

STAMPS

Ryan Chapman

CL Kokomo Coffee (P.101)

The brilliant use of soft shapes and
colours is unmistakable in Ryan Chapman's
illustration. Depicting aquatic life, Denmark
Underwater on this page is one of his recent
attempts to illustrate a country by relevant
activities. On facing page is a set of
stickers designed for Estonian coffee label,
Kokomo Coffee. These cheery stamps form part
of the brand's packaging to mark the African
and South American origins of their four
coffee blends in a delightful way.

ØYENVITNE

Anna Kövecses

CL Øyenvitne

Appearing calm and poetic, these book cover illustrations prelude four new crime novels to be published by Øyenvitne, a Norwegian publishing house whose name translates as "eyewitness". The graphic approach contrasts the usual dark covers that induce a mysterious setting, and intrigues readers in a way that matches the young Scandinavian authors' styles. A logo with a peering face was also conceived, that animates on the publisher's folded business cards.

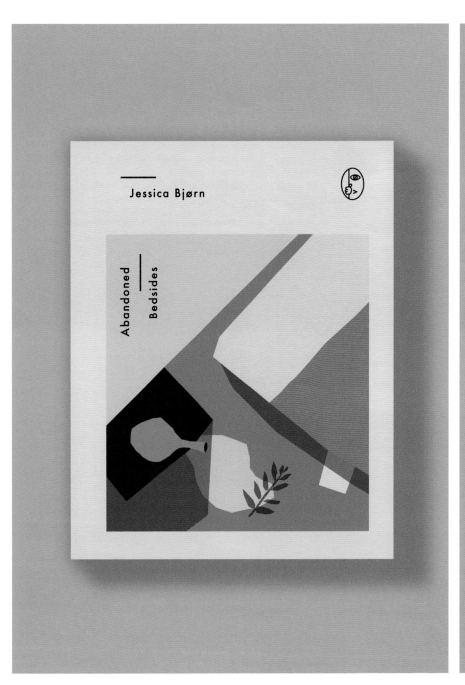

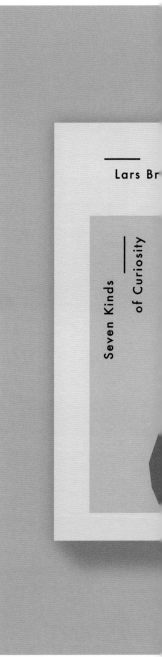

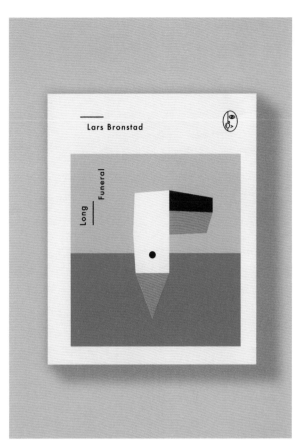

Lars Bronstad

Long Funeral

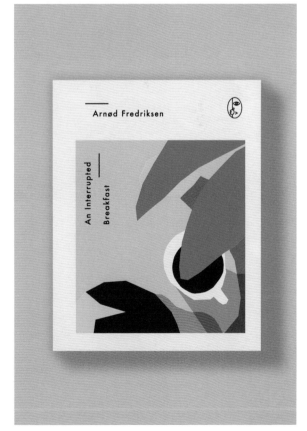

Arnød Fredriksen

An Interrupted Breakfast

NEW FRONTIERS

atelier bingo.

CL New Frontiers

Organised by MA Publishing students at London College of Communication, the 11th Publishing Innovation Conference focused on how stories are told in the media today. Seemingly random elements dance around the event's poster to denote an eclectic programme featuring star speakers involved in various aspects of the current reading culture. Curators, social media specialists, publishers, writers and journalists could all be found in the line-up.

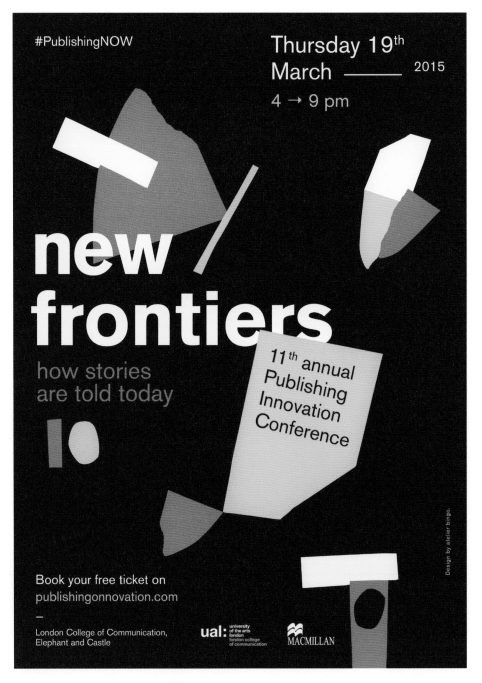

BIOGRAFIAS VIMARANENSES

Non-Verbal Club

PT Margarida Castel-Branco

CL Guimarães 2012 European Capital of Culture

Biografias Vimaranenses contains the life stories and achievements of 12 individuals that occurred in Portuguese city Guimarães. Celebrating individuality and the historical account, a thousand covers were uniquely produced for different copies of the book. Each comprises a varied geometry-based composition singly made by overlaying silkscreen prints, with fluorescent pink to add a contemporary touch.

AGENDA CCCB

Hey

PH Roc Canals
CL CCCB

Centre de Cultura Contemporània de Barcelona (CCCB) publishes a programme guide every two months. Seeing the centre as a receptacle for contemporary ideas, Hey graphically interpreted the cultural centre's building in a profusion of colours and shapes for the 2013 series, that continues to illuminate the booklet's inner pages. The abstract patterns were aimed to create a lasting appeal and invite imagination.

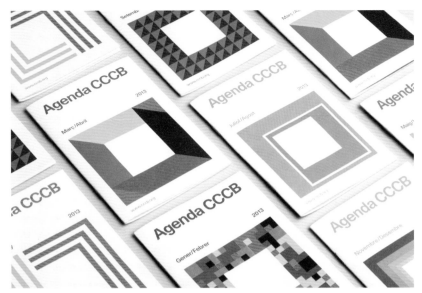

PAUL & MARIGOLD

Foreign Policy Design Group

CL Paul & Marigold

In a set of four, these miniature literature classics affirm Paul & Marigold's affinity with literary work. With a 'hard' cover featuring a gold-foiled book title and decorative lines, these books function as the boutique publishing house's business cards, which unfold the company's contact methods and story over a double-page spread inside. The details were laid out in the style of a book's content page for a complete look.

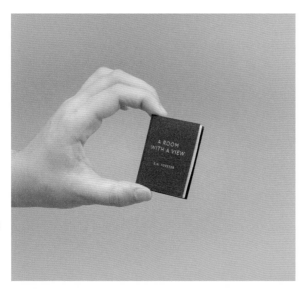
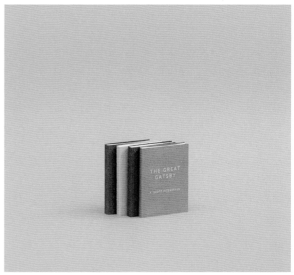

BRAND GUIDE: SINGAPORE EDITION

Foreign Policy Design Group

Foreign Policy has initiated a new project to document the making of 17 iconic Singaporean brands with a multidimensional, analytical approach. The first of their Brand Guide series sets the tone and format of the forthcoming guides, with a kraft paper folder holding brand materials of all sizes and shapes, organising design concepts and process into an informative portfolio that invites exploration. Completely hand-assembled, each guide accents the brand owners and designers' first-hand accounts with personal touches.

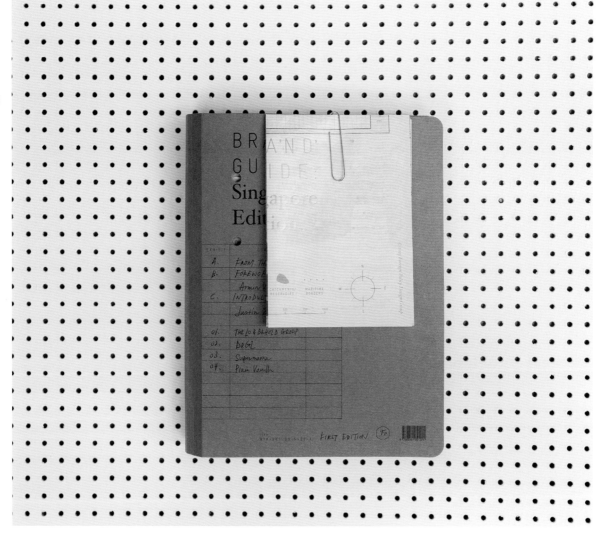

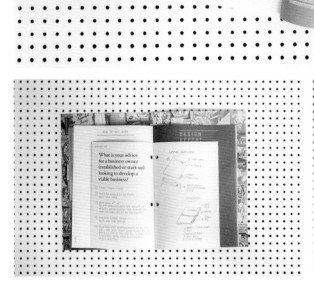

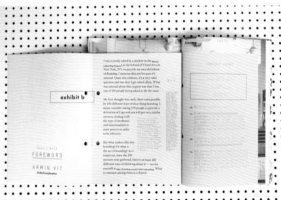

HISTORY OF BRANDING

Strategically located in the heart of Southeast Asia, **Singapore** in its early days attracted strings of immigrants across multiple backgrounds arriving in search of new beginnings. Over the years, this curi-

BRAND
REPORT
(N° 2)

The Lo & Behold Group

Wander lust Hotel

(N° 1) Wanderlust Hotel

DESIGN REPORT

Loosely adapted from the German language, Wanderlust describes a desire to explore new and foreign places in search of an escape or new discoveries. Drawing from this same spirit, Wanderlust Hotel draws from its rich heritage location of Little India as an unexpected location for a hotel to reside in. It encourages travellers to get to know unfamiliar cultures, ways of life, and behaviours present in the ethnic diversity of Singapore.

PLAIN VANILLA
BAKERY

MAP OF
Singapore

BRAND
REPORT
(N°4)

Goodstuph
Museum of Singapore
Working Capitol
DrGL
ng Shunmugam
od For Thought
he Loco Group
n Coffee Roasters
Plain Vanilla
BooksActually
Grafunkt
PACT
Supermama
e Space Program

B R A N D   R E P O R T   (N°1)
Papa Palheta

This story begins with a hero
— the very man who gave this
company its name — Colonel Francisco
de Melo Palheta. In the early 1700s,
the Brazilian colonel was sent
to neighbouring *French Guiana*
to acquire the *prized crop*, and as
some stories go, the officer
charmed the governor's wife into
presenting him with a bouquet of
flowers that contained cuttings
from a *coffee plant*, which fathered the
generations of Brazilian-grown
coffee from that point on.

Strait of Singapore, off the 'S' tip of
nsula.

an independent republic comprising this island and a few adjacent
islets: member of the Commonwealth of Nations; formerly (1826) b
crown colony (1946–59) and member of the federation of Malaysia
(1963–65). 220 sq. mi. (570 sq. km). *Capital* Singapore

a seaport in and the capital of this republic.

Related forms
singaporean, noun, adjective

THE WORKING CAPITOL

Foreign Policy Design Group

CL Bamboo Group

The Working Capitol is a community of knowledge workers who operate at the intersection of creativity, technology, and business. The brand concept was created based on the Euclidean principle which then inspired a visual language, introducing the shared office's goal to provide a beautiful space enhanced by contemporary lifestyle and a community support system. The different permutations of the logo system expand to reflect an intricate and infinite sphere of influence within the space, while a clean, assertive typeface connects with the intelligent minds.

GUIMARÃES JAZZ 2012
POSTERS

Non-Verbal Club

CL Centro Cultural Vila Flor

Going for a solution at variance with the previous year's that vibrantly celebrated Guimarães Jazz Festival's 20th birthday, Non-Verbal Club switched to highlight the musical instruments typically used to play jazz for the festival's 21st edition. Abstractions of drums, saxophones and piano keys frisking around the poster channel the spirit of the music genre, with a vintage look to tribute its golden days. A warm palette finishes off the design, transmitting the geniality that filled jazz musicians and enthusiasts from that era.

> <u>I just look for
> them in
> a different
> way. I'm
> looking for a
> new way to say
> "I love you"</u>.
>
> *Dave Douglas*

J A Z Z

GUIMARÃES JAZZ
8 A 17 — NOV — 2012
CENTRO CULTURAL
VILA FLOR

QUINTA 08 HERBIE HANCOCK - PLUGGED IN. A NIGHT OF SOLO EXPLORATIONS • SEXTA 09
BILL FRISELL / BILL MORRISON:THE GREAT FLOOD • SÁBADO 10 DAVE DOUGLAS & JOE LOVANO
QUINTET: SOUND PRINTS • DOMINGO 11 BIG BAND E ENSEMBLE DE CORDAS DA ESMAE DIRIGIDOS
POR JACAM MANRICKS • DOMINGO 11 LUCIAN BAN ENESCO RE-IMAGINED • QUARTA 14
JACAM MANRICKS BAND • QUINTA 15 PROJETO TOAP/GUIMARÃES JAZZ 2012 | OJM COM MÚSICA DE
JOÃO PAULO ESTEVES DA SILVA • SEXTA 16 THE JAZZ PASSENGERS RE-UNITED • SÁBADO 17
WDR BIG BAND COLOGNE PLAYS THE MUSIC OF RANDY BRECKER

CENTRO CULTURAL VILA FLOR
GUIMARÃES

GUIMARÃES 2012
CAPITAL EUROPEIA DA CULTURA

VINTAGE POSTERS

Mads Berg Illustration

CL Bornholm; On facing page (clockwise) Elsevier magazine, Aiglon Magazine, Air Greenland, Monocle magazine

The harmonic fusion of classic poster design
and modern brand visions are hallmark
features of Mads Berg's illustrations. This
is evident in his work produced to promote
tourism for the island of Bornholm in
Denmark and the posters for Air Greenland,
Elsevier (a Dutch weekly) and Swiss boarding
school Aiglon's magazine. Sometimes Berg
also incorporates messages into his colour
scheme, such as the identity of Denmark that
prevails the cover of Monocle Magazine's
annual national survey.

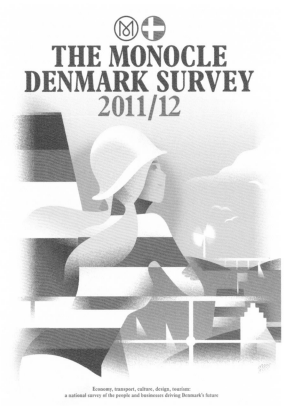

THE MONOCLE
DENMARK SURVEY
2011/12

Economy, transport, culture, design, tourism:
a national survey of the people and businesses driving Denmark's future

ELSEVIER

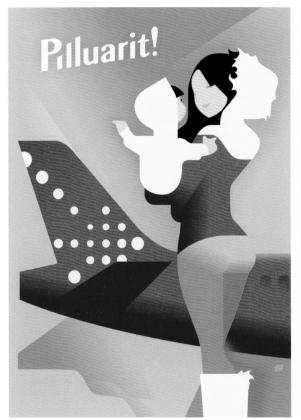

Pilluarit!

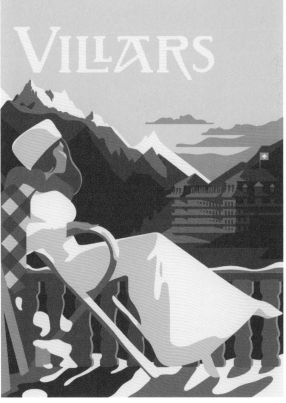

VILLARS

SHOCHIKU MAGAZINE 2015

Motoi Shito

CL Shochiku Co., Ltd

Shochiku's movie productions focus on Japanese dance-drama kabuki. On its 120th anniversary, the company's internal magazine published a special issue, with the number '120' played up and bleeding the cover's rims to heap praise on the company's great achievements. While colours tie glory with Shochiku and the country, a vintage tone alludes to centuries-old national art.

THISWEEK

Motoi Shito

CL THISWEEK

THISWEEK is all about great DJ music set off by visual projections. A graphic rendition of the evening event, these posters foretell its stellar lineup with the name recurring as a party of tricolour blocks and slender typeface to reinforce the unique vibe. The eyes remind viewers that their programme does not only entertain their hearing but also their sights.

SPLIT STONES

Jared Bell

CL Western Vinyl

"Split Stones" originates from the idea of disparate halves coming together — a metaphor for the band and brothers' geographical divide, the dichotomy of rational thoughts and human behaviour, and the organic components derived from electronic music. Noting a vague resemblance to what Surrealist and Metaphysical art manifest, Jared Bell, as one half of the band, explored the curious relationships in a similarly symbolic way.

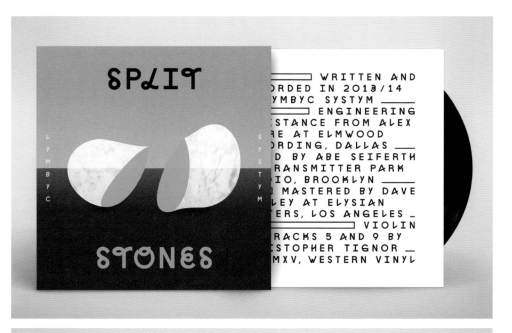

DIMMING AWE, THE LIGHT IS RAW

Jared Bell

CL Western Vinyl

Under the Botany moniker, artist and producer Spencer Stephenson creates danceable and rich psychological tunes. For his second album, *Dimming Awe, The Light is Raw*, Jared Bell interpreted the experimental drone, weaving together geographical abstractions referencing the art of Bauhaus masters Anni Albers and Laszlo Moholy-Nagy alike. The result is a 12-inch vinyl LP packaging with a removable J-card style spine cover that unfolds into a poster.

TRANSIENT SENSES

Pol Pintó Fabregat

CR EINA, Centre Universitari de Disseny i
Art de Barcelona

A site-specific installation created for
Sónar+D, a conference about creativity and
technology, Transient Senses by artist
Alex Arteaga investigates Mies van der
Rohe Pavilion's open-plan design with
visuals, textual and sound. The ephemeral
nature of these elements was graphically
conveyed on the event's collateral, resulting
in a dynamic reflection not to be forgotten.

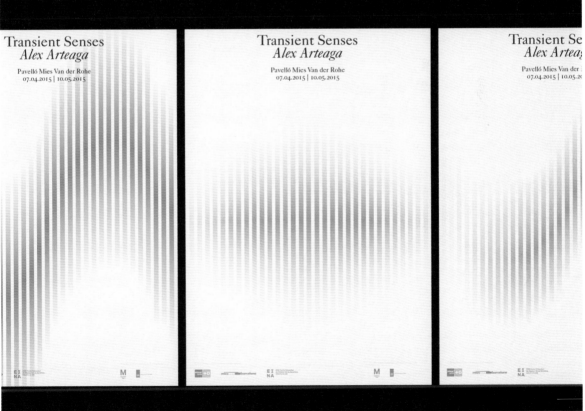

DHUB

Lo Siento

CL DHUB

A set of handouts was produced to promote the opening of Design Museum of Barcelona (DHUB) in 2014. Images of the museum building, collections and text compliment each other in a contrasting tones. All leaflets were produced in poster format, with three fluorescent hues to set apart the different language editions and scream for attention.

ST JAMES'S LONDON
LOCAL AREA GUIDES

dn&co.

IL Katie Scott

PT Push Print

CL The Crown Estate

As part of a placemaking project on St James's, a historic district in central London, four visitor guides were compiled to bring to light the area's core but underrated strengths in food, fashion and art, alongside an everyday amenities guide for local workers. Easy and attractive to read, the guides aim to right out-of-date views with up-to-date reviews and beautiful illustrations. The set is up for grabs at retailers and cultural institutions, each in a characteristic brand colour.

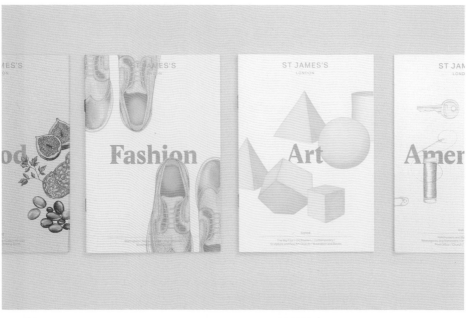

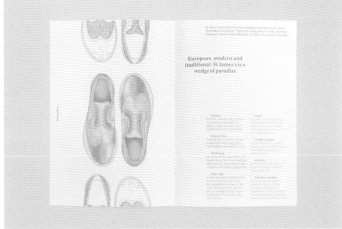

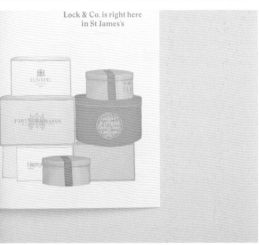

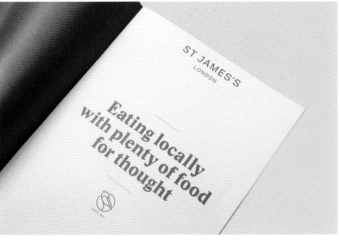

DELICIOUS POSTCARDS

Joe Haddad

PH Darrin Haddad Photography

Sharing is caring — that's why Joe Haddad created Delicious Postcards to log and share the joy of munching a hot sandwich at a classic eatery in New York City on a cold, snowy day. To complete his graphic memory of what he ate and he loves about New York snacks, a rounded plastic type common on special meal boards behind the cashier counters was used to name the item or ingredients on the card's back.

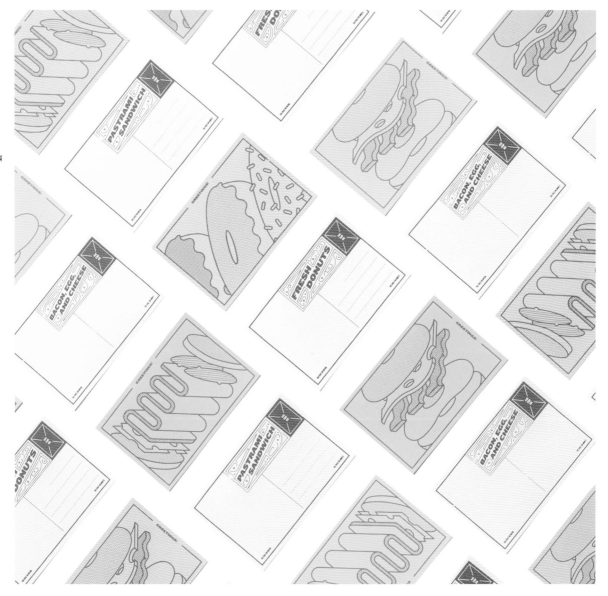

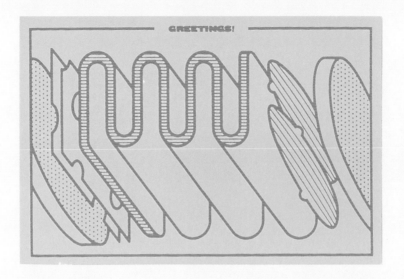

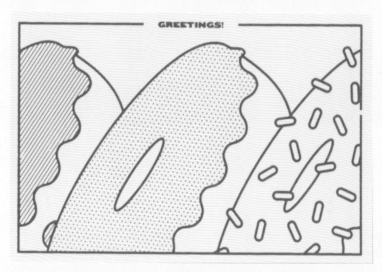

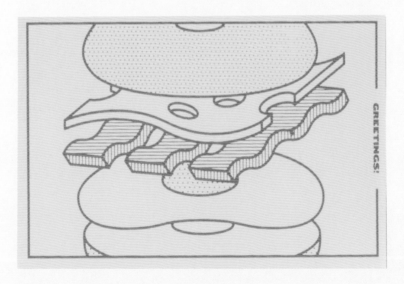

RISOGRAPH PRINTING CALENDAR 2015

O.OO Risograph Printing & Design ROOM

In an edition of 200, the six-page calendar
has come as the result of Risograph
printing experimentation. Using seven colour
ink, the stencil duplication process created
subtle nuances of lines, shapes and colour
layers, leading to absolutely unique designs
on every print. Perforated lines made for
a thoughtful addition, allowing users to
tear off the colourful prints for collection
after every two months.

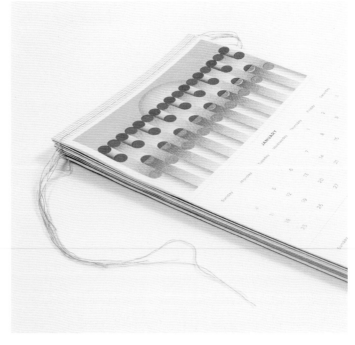

UNFINISHED DAYDREAM

0.00 Risograph Printing & Design ROOM

Playing with visual texture, colours, shapes and line patterns, Unfinished Daydream was carried out to manifest the potential of Risograph printing. With colours limited to orange, blue and green, these illustrations reveal interesting interactions between colour patches and graphic elements of various volume and densities. The prints were produced in poster and postcard formats for enjoyment.

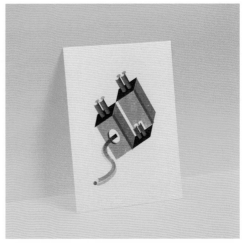

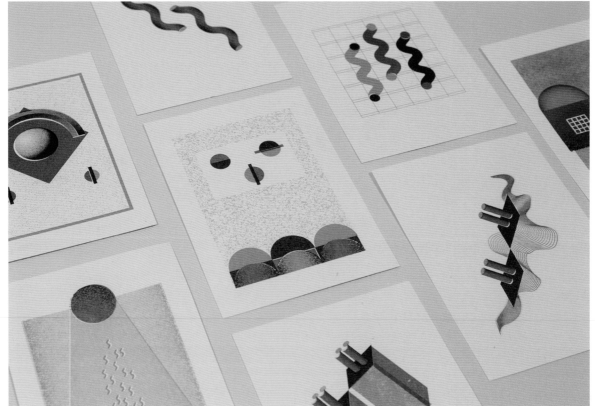

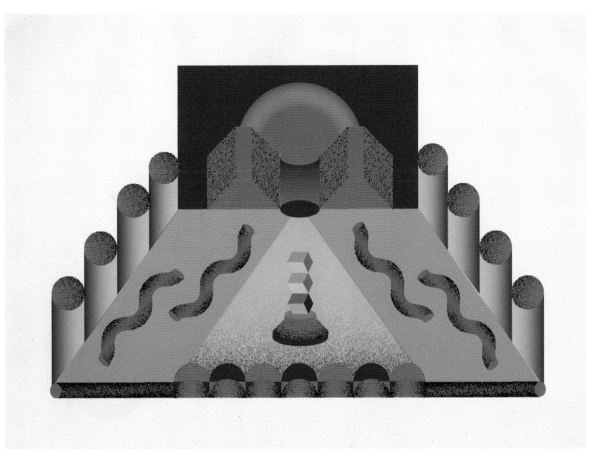

CIRCA

Bunker3022

PH Magali Seberian

CL Circa

Circa specialises in fabric print design. To demonstrate their commitment to bringing joy through their bold, beautiful prints, the Argentine company's brand identity unifies these elements into a coherent and communicative language, through a collage of archive images, modern patterns and Circa's hallmark prints. A warm palette reinforces the idea across its business cards and packaging bags.

KIXBOX SS14 SAMPLE SALE

Facultative Works

CL Kixbox

Whether these illustrations depicted a real or fictional post-apocalyptic scene, Kixbox will let Russia's cool crowd find out at its multi-label boutiques. Made to announce the store's limited-time sample sale, these images winnow out the cliché marketing tag lines and intrigue viewers by imagining what would happen as nuclear winter arrives. Every street wear item help reveal a corner of an emptied flat and an episode of the story.

KIXBOX

SS/14

ГОЛОВНЫЕ

УБОРЫ _____ 269

KIXBOX

SS/14

PENFIELD _____ 539

KIXBOX

SS/14

UNDFTD _____ 67

KIXBOX

SS/14

РУБАШКИ

ПОЛО _____ 449

KIXBOX

SS/14

ПЛАТЬЯ _____ 53

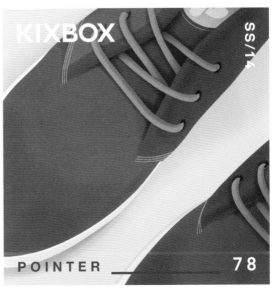

KIXBOX

SS/14

POINTER _____ 78

SÉRIGRAPHIE ULDRY
COMPLIMENT CARDS

A3 Studio

PT,CL Sérigraphie Uldry

A3 Studio designed a set of A5-size
complimentary cards for Swiss silkscreen
printer, Sérigraphie Uldry. A nod to the
printer's expertise, a silk screen squeegee
dominates the card with the printer's name
recurring in the background. Only three
coloured inks were employed and a number of
variants was brought about for use.

TIMELESS, MASSIMO VIGNELLI

A3 Studio

CL Husmee

"Timeless, Massimo Vignelli" is a collective exhibition that celebrates designer Massimo Vignelli's aesthetic influences on modern life. A3 Studio is among the 30 some units invited to create a graphic tribute to the late master. The result is a potpourri of iconic logos created by Vignelli, that strips down to their pure coloured shapes in absence of names and words. These shapes feature logos of the American Airlines, Benetton, Cinzano, Bloomingdales and New York subway's signage system.

B*THERE FESTIVAL 2014

Studio Daad, Studio Turbo

CL B*THERE Festival

B*THERE is an annual two-day festival of art, music and culture that takes place in Dutch city, 's-Hertogenbosch. Keen on drawing the public's immediate attention to what was about to unfold during the event, the designers drew on the warning sign language typical of the ones used in a construction sits. The raw sticks and hand-painted finishing gave off a edgy DIY feel across the posters, flyers, invitations and many more.

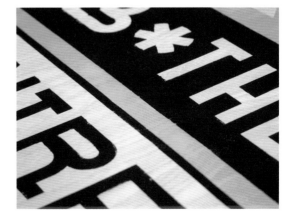

PAPA PALHETA BRAND
EXPERIENCE KIT

Foreign Policy Design Group

CL Papa Palheta

The Papa Palheta experience kit is designed to engage customers in coffee culture and manifest the specialty coffee brand's strong coffee roots down to sustainability. Apart from a bag for redeeming bean samples, the kit consists of a set of cards — one made from disposed coffee chaff to encourage repurposing, a coffee tasting note, a brewing guide and a cake recipe for pairing. Geometric shapes, fluorescent colours and assorted paper stock generate a sensory experience that transcends the common brown coffee packaging.

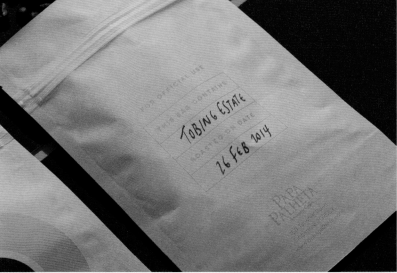

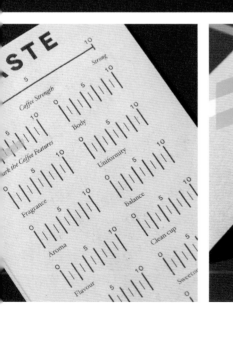

HUNGARIAN INVENTORS SERIES

Absoloot

CD,DE,IL Eszter Csontos

PH Nóra Puskás, Bertalan Bessenyey

CL Magma Gallery, Budapest

Commissioned by Magma Gallery, Hungarian Inventors is an exhibition memorabilia made to commemorate the late Hungarian originators who had contribute incredible improvements to modern life. Simple to the eye but impressive by touch, the colourless Hungarian folk art motifs on the packaging box connote how their invention of ballpoint pens and refrigerators appears to the world today. Illustrated portraits and handwritings hint at the epoch where these products came to life.

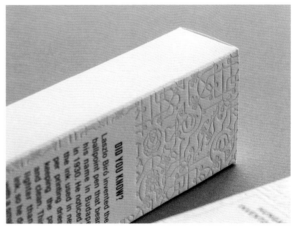

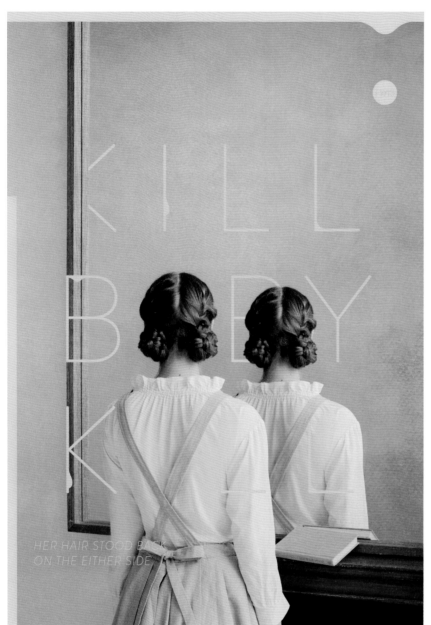

HER HAIR STOOD BACK
ON THE EITHER SIDE

CLOSE THE DOOR
AND CUT INTO HALF

KILL BABY KILL

studiowmw

PH Missbean

CL röyksopp gakkai

Drawing inspirations from horror films in the 1970s and 1980s and classical European children clothing as the brand's signature, röyksopp gakkai's 2015 Fall/Winter collection's theme is "a nightmare dressed like a daydream". Enveloped in a sleeve with a die-cut window, the mailers feature styling shots that aim to provoke an eerie atmosphere as if one is looking out of a window in a haunted mansion.

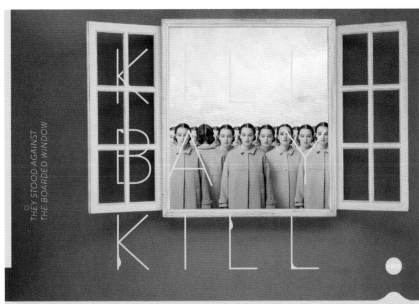

THEY STOOD AGAINST
THE BOARDED WINDOW

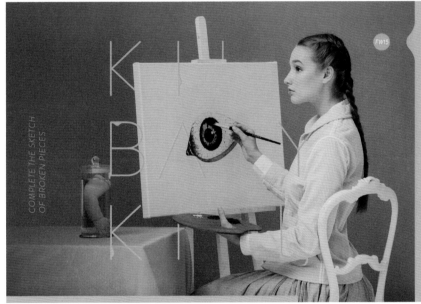

COMPLETE THE SKETCH
OF BROKEN PIECES

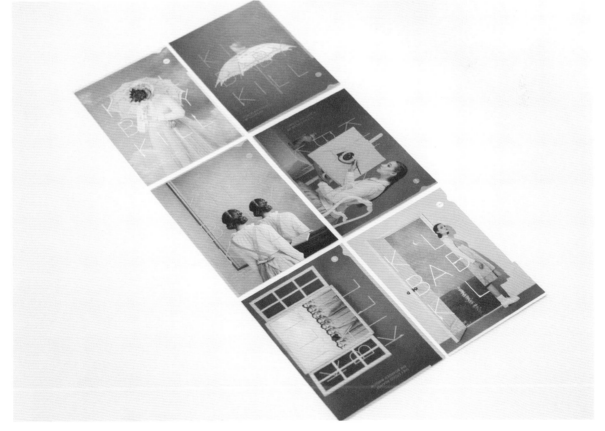

FFF-ACCURATE TOOL

Fundamental Studio

CL Overlab

FFF is short for "form follows function", the design principle that underlies Fundamental Studio's work. Coming about as the first collaboration between Fundamental and letterpress printer, Overlab, the postcard manifests the key design approach and Overlab's superb techniques by analogy with a vernier calliper. The printer materialised the idea tangibly by print.

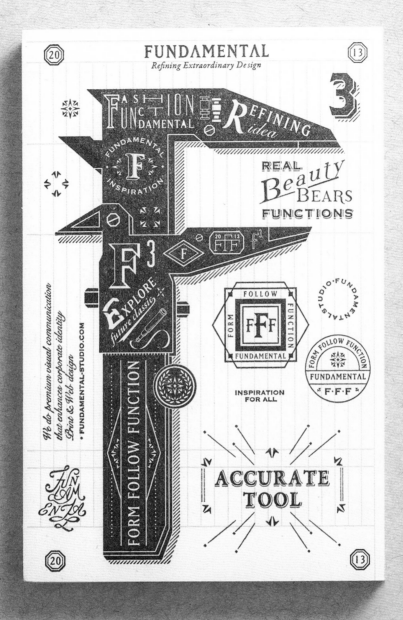

COCOA COLONY

Bravo

CL KOP

The brand Cocoa Colony is inspired by the brothers who brought cocoa beans from Colonial Ecuador to Europe. Tracing the long forgotten benefits of consuming cocoa beans, Cocoa Colony's graphic identity uses enormous gold elements to hark back to a time when the beans were referred to as "Amazonian Gold" for its healing properties. The typographic choice and the materiality of its brand elements both play a part in retelling the story.

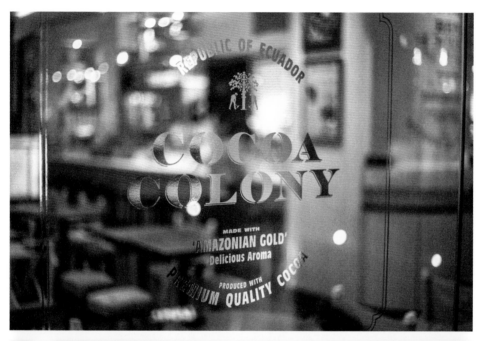

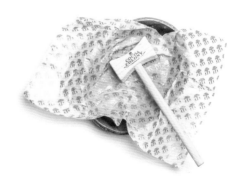

CAPPAN STUDIO

Zealplus

CL CAPPAN STUDIO

Branding for printer CAPPAN STUDIO salutes letterpress as a traditional printing technique which they strive to perfect with recourse to the latest technology. Typography is integral to CAPPAN's logo and visual identity design, denoting their adherence to printing with movable types. Juxtaposing classic typefaces with a modified letter 'C', ZEALPLUS ensured the idea of tradition and modernity play equal parts in the brand.

FOE

Oddds

CL Penguin Books

Oddds was asked to design the cover of *Foe (1986)* by J.M. Coetzee. To be published by Penguin Books as part of the 'Penguin Essentials', the cult classic was part of the satirical retelling of Robinson Crusoe, a historical fiction woven around the mariner's strange adventures. The final design was produced in the fashion of a vintage navigation map, picturing mutiny, voyage and death that centre the fiction's plot.

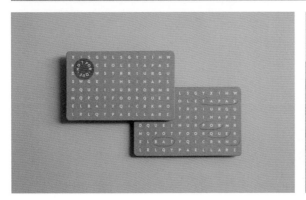

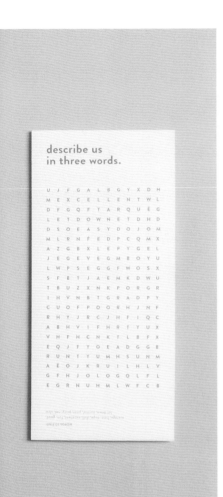

¿POR QUÉ NO?

Table Six

CL ¿Por Qué No?

¿Por Qué No? is a Spanish restaurant in Jakarta committed to topping off their tapas dishes with glee. Brand applications embrace the spirit throughout, with formats and graphics all incorporating the idea of "games". Mostly old-time games, such as crosswords and puzzles, in colours comprised of natural materials and a passionate red, the designs connect dining experience at ¿Por Qué No? with the typical Spanish hospitality and authentic tastes which the restaurant lays stress on.

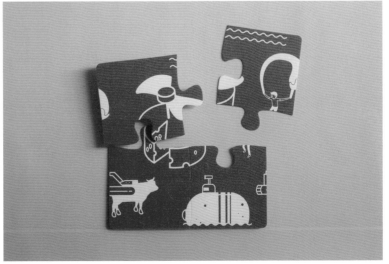

SCOUTING UNIT

Table Six

CL Scouting Unit

Scouting Unit sells daily goods that come as a collaboration between design house Table Six and selected artists, designers and manufacturers. Translating an approach that roots deep in functionality and beauty, Scouting Unit's identity positions the online store as a blank canvas where future products to perform their goodness. Muted colours and a pared-down design reiterates these values as well as confidence in their aesthetic judgement.

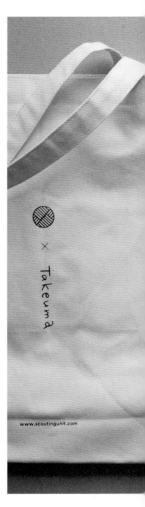

Think "Bitter"　Think "Sweet"

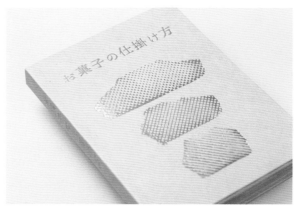

H.C.CREATION INITIATION CATALOGUE

UMA/design farm

CP Paradox creative Inc.

PH Yoshiro Masuda

CL H.C.Création Co., Ltd.

Three perfectly baked financiers and a delicate brand book vividly present Japanese patisserie, H.C.Creation's dedication to their potential employees. Where colourful pictures and text detail their manufacturing approach and philosophies, a gold-foiled mark repeats on the kit, bringing their baking process and a sense of quality to the fore. The line "Think 'bitter' think 'sweet'" is added to prompt young job seekers to view the cakes with a business mind.

A-CREIXEMENT

Pol Pintó Fabregat

CR EINA, Centre Universitari de Disseny i
Art de Barcelona

Pol Pintó Fabregat has made a critical
comment on today's consumer capitalism as his
graduation project at EINA, University School
of Design and Art. Titled "A-creixement",
which translates as A-growth, and featuring
a reversion motif, the campaign quietly

calls for an insurrection and slams
visual-based marketing techniques with a
typographic approach. To help spread the
message, a rubber stamp makes it easy
to transform any mediums into effective
campaign materials.

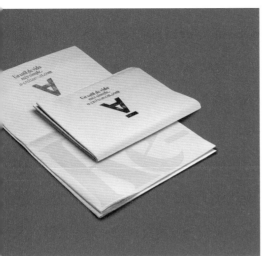

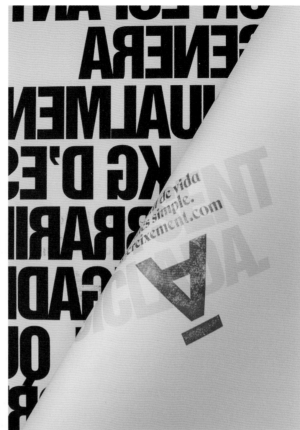

GOOD OLD DAYS

O.OO Risograph Printing & Design ROOM

PH Chang Chieh

Good Old Days honours letter writing and the beauty of Risograph prints. A cue for people to pick up a pen and write, retro graphics were applied to quality letter paper and the packaging box, bringing to mind a sense of sophistication and the grace of writing the age-old practice stands for. Decked with gold printing, each letter writing box contains six sets of letter sheets and envelopes alongside a complimentary postcard.

PORTES OUVERTES
DE LA CITÉ 2014

A3 Studio

CL Portes ouvertes de la Cité

Every December, the city of Lausanne hosts Portes ouvertes de la Cité to engage the public to rediscover the charm of La Cité, an old part of town. A graphical interpretation of the event's programmes, open doors intermingle with the area's name, transmitting a sense of movement and dynamism. The varied door designs suggest the diversity of shops and museums participating in the event. A colour scheme made of blue, gold and white corresponds to the festive season.

KISSTHEDESIGN INVITATION

A3 Studio

CL Kissthedesign Gallery

Kissthedesign Gallery's fifth anniversary party was all about celebrating the number "5". The number becomes a graphic and numeral leitmotif in the party invitation design, with the message broken into five rows of five letters, spreading evenly over a pattern made of 5s. The gallery made its presence felt on the card in its corporate colour, black and pink.

JOURNÉES DES ALTERNATIVES URBAINES 2015

A3 Studio

CL Journées des alternatives urbaines

"Les Journées des alternatives urbaines" seeks to make creative ideas and experiment activities around social innovation and development visible in the city. The theme of its year 2015 edition was "Do It Together". Laying stress on a concerted effort to develop solutions and practices, the poster campaign visualises this collective dynamics as two clasped hands symbolically forming an interactive chain.

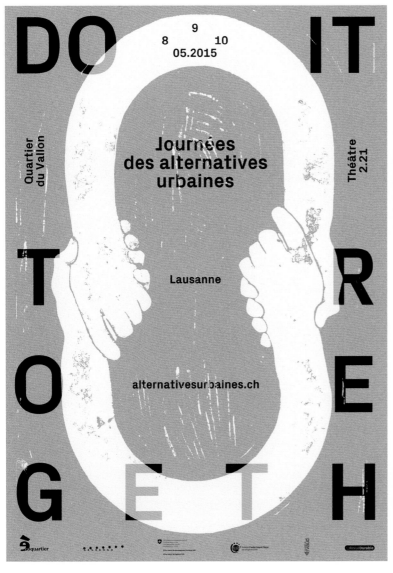

DESIGN DAYS 2011

A3 Studio

CL Association Design Days

Organised by interior design magazine Espaces
Contemporains, Design Days celebrates
contemporary furniture design. In search for
a strong element to define the annual event,
A3 made the letter D as the identity's focal
point with a folded design to give the logo
a more technical aspect. The posters were
designed as a set of two, reminiscent of
1950's Swiss graphic design. When paired side
by side, the bold yellow strokes assemble an
"A" as the magazine's mark.

DESIGN DAYS 2014

A3 Studio

~~~~~~~~~~~~~~~~~~~~~~~~~~~~~~~~~~~
CL Association Design Days

Referencing last century's Modernist graphic style, the visual identity of Design Days's 2014 edition manifests a resolutely minimalist spirit. Plain colours, a serif Swiss typeface, gradient and geometric shapes keep the language precise, drawing audience's attention back to the very essence of design. The Ds taken from the event's name intertwine to signify the absence of boundaries within design.

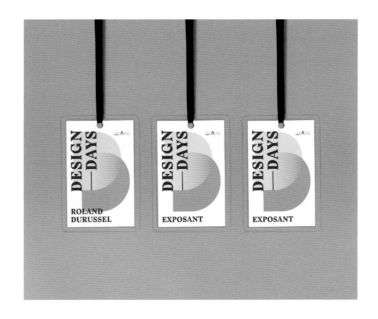

HVALSTRANDFESTIVALEN

Commando Group

CL Håland, Eidsvåg & Strøm

Loud and compelling, Hvalstrandfestivalen's identity draws on maritime signal flags and codes to tie the event with its picturesque seaside venue. The music festival welcomes an audience of all ages, inspiring an adorable tricolour design with a varied geometric pattern boosting a party vibe across its tickets, mementos and decoration. The design is set to evolve year by year. A playful typeface completes the concept on a pleasant note.

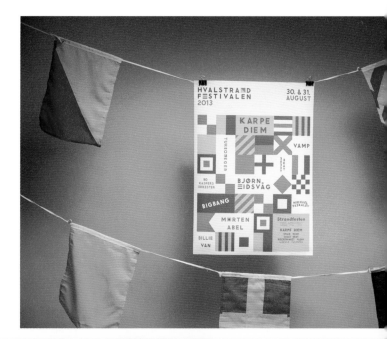

ART.FAB.LAB

innoise

CL K11 Hong Kong

ART.FAB.LAB is a makers' workshop, exhibition and seminar space rolled into one. Focusing on digital fabrication and its role in art and design, the event offered a platform where artists and the public can interact and get to know the new model of local production with die-cutting and 3D printing techniques. With a recurring motif, the visual system aims to extend a warm welcome and lure passers-by to the event.

ART.FAB.LAB.

YOU CAN MAKE (ALMOST) EVERYTHING!

PRESENTED BY dimension+ CO-ORGANISED BY K11 Lab BY DIMENSION+

FRANÇOIS BRUMENT AND
SONIA LAUGIER (FRANCER 法國)
FABRAFT DESIGN LAB 衍象設計 (TAIWAN 台灣)
LUKE JERRAM (UNITED KINGDOM 英國)
EDDY HUI 許迅 (HONG KONG 香港)
YOUNGHUI KIM (KOREAR 韓國)
KEITH LAM 林欣傑 (HONG KONG 香港)
KIM LAM (HONG KONG 香港)
LIA (AUSTRIA 奧地利)
GERARD RUBIO (SPAIN 西班牙)
WONG TING YAN 王天仁 (HONG KONG 香港)

K11 ART SPACE

14.MAR-17.MAY2015

ART.FAB.LAB.

YOU CAN MAKE (ALMOST) EVERYTHING!

ART. FAB. LAB.

ART.FAB.LAB.

14.MAR-17.MAY2015
K11 ART SPACE
THOUGH B2 D-MOP ZONE / MTR EXIT N3
經 B2 D-MOP ZONE 入 / 港鐵 N3出口

FRANÇOIS BRUMENT AND
SONIA LAUGIER (FRANCE 法國)
FABRAFT DESIGN LAB 衍象設計 (TAIWAN 台灣)
LUKE JERRAM (UNITED KINGDOM 英國)
EDDY HUI 許迅 (HONG KONG 香港)
YOUNGHUI KIM (KOREA 韓國)
KEITH LAM 林欣傑 (HONG KONG 香港)
KIM LAM (HONG KONG 香港)
LIA (AUSTRIA 奧地利)
GERARD RUBIO (SPAIN 西班牙)
WONG TING YAN 王天仁 (HONG KONG 香港)

ART.FAB.LAB.

K11 ART MALL
18 HANOI ROAD
TSIM SHA TSUI
KOWLOON
HONG KONG
K11 ART SPACE
K11 購物藝術館
香港九龍尖沙咀河內道18號

ART.
FAB.
LAB.

DESIGNED BY INNOISE

YOU CAN MAKE (ALMOST) EVERYTHING!

PEAR ECO
Futura

Pear Eco

CL A. Roland Row

Pear Eco is an Australian organic food label in Taiwan. An earthy tone, kraft paper and a no-frills design call attention to its product's sheer quality rooted in its all- natural and handmade nature. Together with the metallic finishing and a leaf-shaped tag, the visual identity injects credibility into Pear Eco's brand image that speaks to the increasingly health-conscious consumer market.

DÉ-CONNECTONS

Claire Susie Jane

CR Le Corbusier - School of Architecture,
Construction and Design

Dé-connectons aimed to raise public
awareness of the consequences of smartphone
addiction. Taking on a more casual tone,
Claire Susie Jane's idea was to prompt self-
reflection through humour and games. Card
game, stamp and protocol book were provided
to help players invent their own solutions to
the highlighted problems or simply discuss it
in groups.

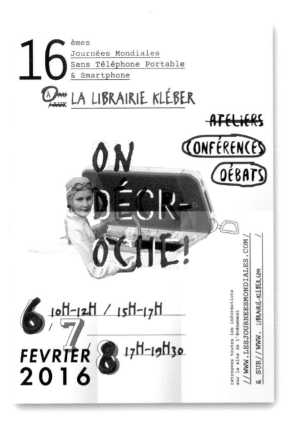

16 èmes
Journées Mondiales
Sans Téléphone Portable
& Smartphone

À / AU / AUX LA LIBRAIRIE KLÉBER

ATELIERS
CONFÉRENCES
DÉBATS

ON DÉCR-OCHE!

6 10H-12H / 15H-17H
7
8 17H-19H30

FEVRIER
2016

retrouvez toutes les informations
sur le site de l'événement
& SUR// WWW. LIBRAIRIE-KLEBER.COM /

16 èmes
Journées Mondiales
Sans Téléphone Portable
& Smartphone

À / AU / AUX LA MÉDIATHÈQUE MALRAUX

ATELIERS
CONFÉRENCES
DÉBATS

ON DÉCR-OCHE!

6 DE 13H30 À 17H30
7
8 DÈS 16H

FEVRIER
2016

retrouvez toutes les informations
sur le site de l'événement
// WWW.LESJOURNEESMONDIALES.COM /
& SUR// WWW. MEDIATHEQUES-CUS.FR /

16 èmes
Journées Mondiales
Sans Téléphone Portable
& Smartphone

À / AU / AUX SÉRIES-GRAPHIQUES

ATELIERS
CONFÉRENCES
(DÉBATS)

ON DÉCR-OCHE!

6 DE 14H30 À 17H
7 DE 16H30 À 18H30
8

FEVRIER
2016

retrouvez toutes les informations
sur le site de l'événement
// WWW.LESJOURNEESMONDIALES.COM /
& SUR// WWW. SERIES-GRAPHIQUES.COM /

16 èmes
Journées Mondiales
Sans Téléphone Portable
& Smartphone

À / AU / AUX SHADOK

ATELIERS
CONFÉRENCES
DÉBATS

ON DÉCR-OCHE!

6 À PARTIR DE 10H - JUSQU'À 15H
7 DE 10H À MIDI
8 DE 17H À 18H30

FEVRIER
2016

retrouvez toutes les informations
sur le site de l'événement
// WWW.LESJOURNEESMONDIALES.COM /
& SUR// WWW. SHADOK.STRASBOURG.EU /

MOONSTONE
CREATIVE STUDIO

HYPE Studio

CL MoonStone Creative Studio

MoonStone Creative Studio is an independent apparel and creative goods brand from Hanoi, Vietnam. The label's logo revives the design of old-time trademarks and features a devilish rabbit as mascot ringed in MoonStone's name and establishment year. In keeping with its cool boy look, the brand's stationery and packaging adopt a solemn duo tone palette set off by gold-foiled details.

MUSETTE BAKERY

Judit Besze

Branding for Musette Bakery emphasises on
the sheer quality of their tasty bread and
pastries. The visual packaging traces the
reason back to its traditional practices,
with craft paper suggestive of the rustic
charm of their freshly-baked bread and a
chequer design evocative of a conventional
home kitchen where the products are
prepared. An upright type and a neutral
palette run through the design with a hint
of authenticity.

SEAFARERS

Inhouse Design

CL Northwest Holdings

A brand overhaul has been conceived for Seafarers Building in Auckland's Britomart precinct following a major renovation in 2014. Before being modernised as an entertainment and business hub, the 1970s building was home to global maritime welfare charity, The Mission to Seafarers, which gives it its name. The new identity also honours its past, reflecting a close tie with the nautical culture running from its emblem to its environmental graphics with a vintage flair.

PIVOVARNA 1713

Milos Milovanovic

CL 1713 Pivovarna d.o.o - Tadej Feregotto

Slovenian micro-brewery Pivovarna 1713 is
named after the 1713 Tolmin peasant revolt
that took place near the brewery's location
at the Soča Valley. Asked to build a brand
to reference the historical uprising that
speaks to drinkers aged around 18-25, Milos
Milovanovic created The Bloody Executioner,
Cheating Tax Collector, Rebellious Peasant
and Greedy Emperor to represent each beer
type. Like the beer, everyone has an
outstanding character, with visual cues
tracing back to the 18th century world.

HOTEL TROFANA ALPIN

Bureau Rabensteiner

CL Nadine Von der Thannen

Trofana Alpin is a traditional family-run hotel in Ischgl, a popular ski destination in Austria. Bureau Rabensteiner was commissioned to modernise the hotel's brand and has aimed for a look and feel that focuses on their exemplary ability to promote tradition with comfort, convenience and spare elegance. Where a balance was achieved by mixing vintage images, woodcut-style illustrations and a clean type, the presence of wood suggests the hotel's proximity to the woods.

LE PAIN BOULE

artless Inc.

CL YAMATO co. Ltd.

Branding and the package design for Japanese artisanal bakery Le pain Boule was crafted to embrace the refined sensibility of the artisans. The delicate flavour of the baked goods made from carefully selected ingredients is graphically translated into a tidy script and an upright functional type "Brandon" which, together with kraft paper, adds warmth and tactility to the brand. Royal blue complements the down-to-earth character with understated sophistication.

RED KAP

Perky Bros, redpepper

Workwear manufacturer Red Kap asked for
a lasting imprint to impress the 300
distributors to coincide with the
introduction of their new Crew Shirt.
Instead of a standard sample descriptions,
stories were told, by 300 hard-working
target wearers who tested the shirt and
shared their experience first hand.
The legitimacy of these taken steps is
encapsulated in handwriting and individual
stories on the tag and stamps, turning the
item into a powerful marketing tool.

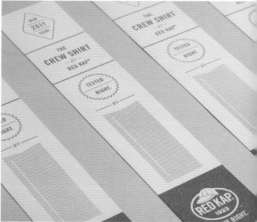

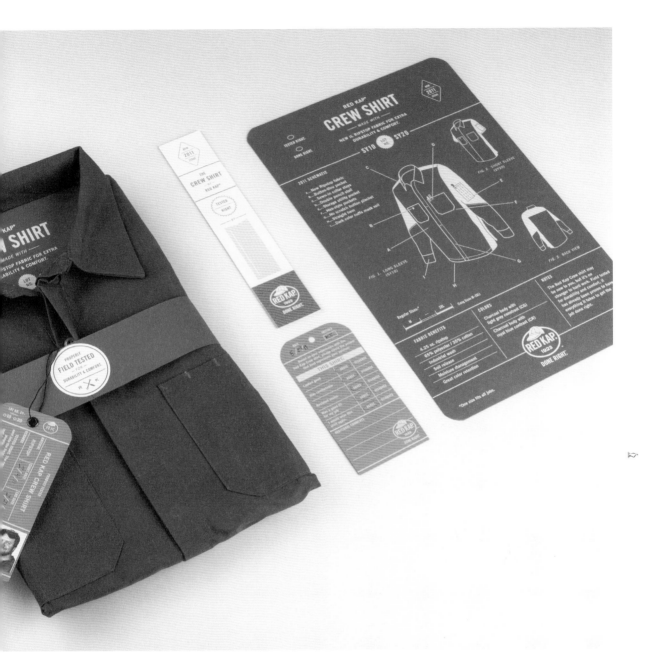

TENDERLOIN MUSEUM

Mucho

CL Tenderloin Museum

The Tenderloin Museum is committed to chronicling the rich history of the San Francisco neighbourhood once peopled by immigrants and iconoclasts, artists and activists, sinners and saints. The visual identity for the museum captures the area's storied past, with mixed type styles borrowed from classic street signs and shop signs evocative of "girls, gambling and graft". A woodblock font further illustrates the gritty nature of Tenderloin, resulting in an eclectic identity that only the museum could own.

ZACH & RACHEL

Yondr Studio

CL Zachary & Rachel Yoder

Having designed wedding invitations for three of his sisters, Nathan Yoder kept this "family tradition" up and running by doing the same for his little brother. Bringing his specialty of illustration and lettering into play, he originated an invite in a

retro design with pen and ink which is later realised in offset lithograph. Hand drawn portraits of the bride and groom-to-be and its surrounding variegated lettering compose a layout with visual richness that exudes festivity.

BEE & BLOOM

Yondr Studio

CL Bee & Bloom

Beekeeping and healthy eating blog Bee & Bloom manifests that simplicity originates quality of life. To this end, the blog's visual identity was kept to a minimal, dominated by three stripes and a transfigured ampersand sign to reference a bee and convey the idea of the focus on natural lifestyle. Monochrome print and the use of unbleached paper cohere with the idea in a neat and simple way.

Cont. Net. 750 ml

MEZCAL JOVEN 100% AGAVE

48% Alc.

Envasado por:
Emiliano Vargas Frías
Paseo Bolívar 612,
Zona Centro
Chihuahua, Chih.
RFC. VAFE741116AP7

El abuso al consu
producto es noc
salud.

Hecho en M

Extraído en

DELINCUENTE

Estudio Yeyé

Delincuente produces mezcal, a native liquor from Mexico. Referencing the beverage's origin and the nation's notable high crime rate, the packaging solution honours drug trades and poverty with an economic wrapper where quirky hybrids and semi-transparent overlays create a hallucinating effect of drugs on a user. A logo featuring morphing faces and tally marks vaguely suggestive of crime figures reinforces the concept.

GUIMARÃES JAZZ 2011
POSTERS

Non-Verbal Club

IL Aleksandra Niepsuj
CL Centro Cultural Vila Flor

Strikingly infectious, Guimarães Jazz 2011's poster design celebrated both the return of the Portuguese music festival and its 20th birthday at once. Futurism and Dada influences were key to what Non-Verbal Club had in mind, who then collaborated with illustrator Aleksandra Niepsuj, who helped bring a certain naivety to the contrasting look the designers wanted to express. The result was three enthusiastic designs, each engaging in a visually rhythmic way.

FORMOSA MEDICINE SHOW

Onion Design Associates

CL The Muddy Basin Ramblers

The Muddy Basin Ramblers is a Taiwanese jug band specialising in old time jazz, blues and ragtime. With their album's concept rooted in 1920s local medicine shows, Onion Design put forward a solution that stays true to the illustrated bilingual ads popular at the time. Titled "Formosa Medicine Show", the album is wrapped in a 45-RPM sleeve, completed with a vintage classified-ad looking design that unfolds the song's lyrics.

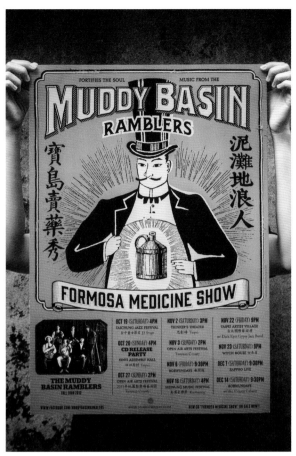

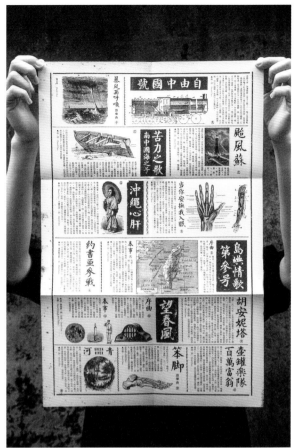

THE ADVERTISEMENT SAYS

Wang Zhi-Hong Studio

CL Rye Field Publications

Titled "The Advertisement Says", the book examines modern Taiwanese life through advertisements arose during Japanese colonial rule. In an attempt to evoke how old brands, trendy products and strategic marketing campaigns overpower consumers, Wang put together a tabloid-size jacket where a chaotic mass of archived print graphics almost buries the book's title. Each piece picked makes for an exquisite showcase of vintage illustrations, text arrangement and logos that Wang holds dear.

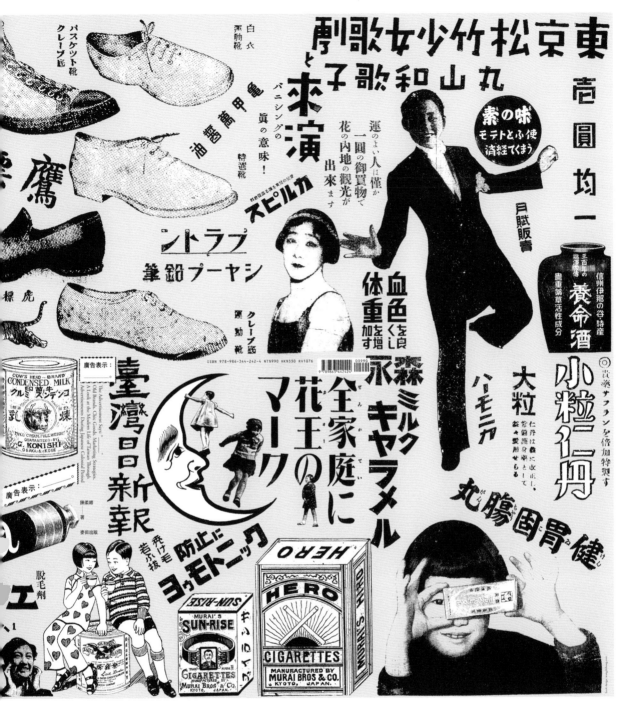

SPARKLE STUDIO

Violaine & Jérémy

PH Olivia Fremineau
CL Sparkle

Sparkle Studio is a creative partnership between music producers David Dahan and Joseph Guigui. Driven to contrive contemporary soundscapes with rare vintage equipment, the Parisian music production studio conceived a basic diamond-shaped logo with a prominent vintage quality to match the name "Sparkle" that can be used alone or paired with the owners in their very nice suits. The intricate illustrations add a fashionable touch.

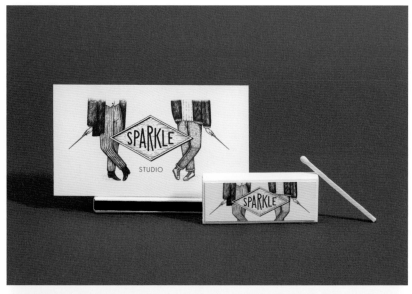

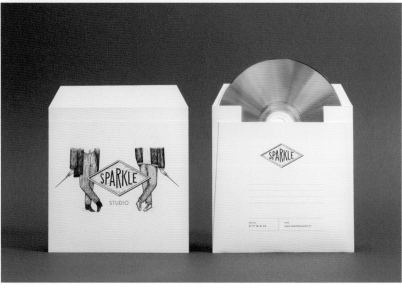

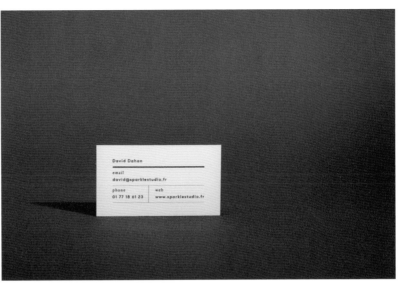

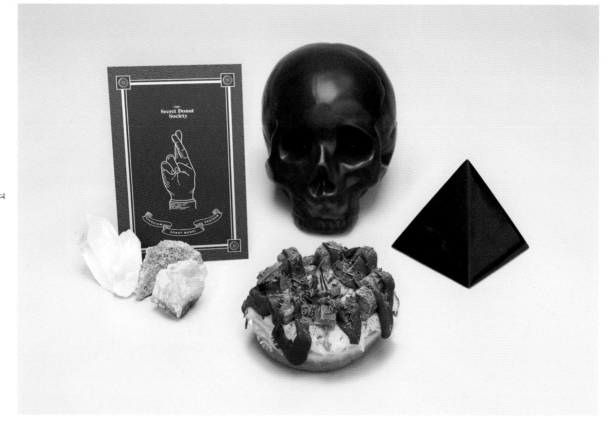

THE SECRET DONUT SOCIETY

Ceci Peralta, José Velázquez

A hidden gem in San Pedro Garza Garcia, The Secret Donut Society sells donuts characterised by bold flavours ensconced in a basement. The store is named by designers Ceci Peralta and José Velázquez, who also developed its brand identity that sustains the business' eccentric charisma. Referencing the Masons and Illuminati, the duo created a visual identity system that would mesmerise donut buffs.

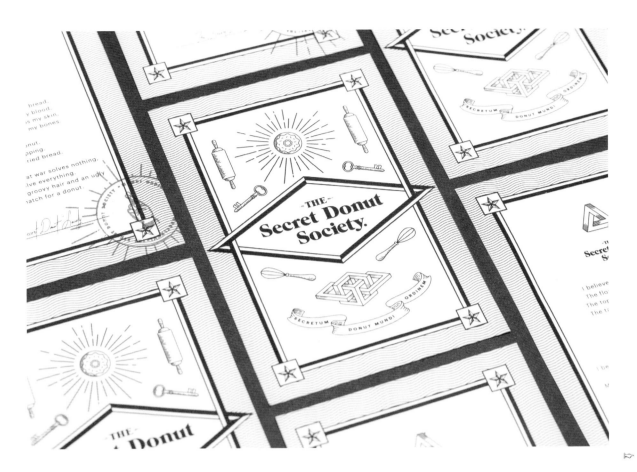

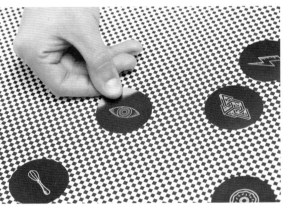

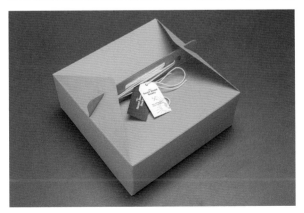

THE CLIFFORD PIER

Foreign Policy Design Group

CL The Clifford Pier

Named from the bustling port at Marina Bay in the 1930s, The Clifford Pier is a Singapore-based restaurant serving contemporary Southeast Asian cuisine. The port's legacy was a major inspiration for the restaurant's visual identity, with a ginger flower motif to honour the country's botany that once fascinated General William Farquhar during his stay on the island. Classic postage stamps, sea-trip elements, a marine-inspired palette and food illustrations resembling Farquhar's remarkable collection of natural history drawings round up the idea as an homage to the historic waterfront landmark.

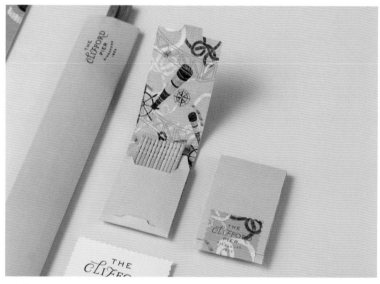

HAYMARKET

Foreign Policy Design Group

CL Hong Kong Jockey Club

Nestled in a British colonial establishment, HayMarket is a meeting point of horse-racing spectators at Hong Kong's Shatin Racecourse. The restaurant's visual identity system is an eclectic mix of vintage British typography, Victorian illustrations commonly found in old advertisements and vibrant graphics that drew on the jockey culture. The logo is a playful update on classic letterforms and functions as a blank canvas, allowing for quirky permutations when combined with different illustrations.

THE LADIES' PURSE
HAPPY VALLEY RACECOURSE

WEDNESDAY, FEBRUARY 25TH, 1863

HOTSPUR v. YEDDO

The Unique Prize
PONY ENTRANCE FEE $5

A Purse with 21 Sovereigns
PRESENTED BY MISS POLLARD

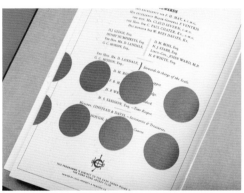

EL CAMINO FOODTRUCK

Savvy Studio

PH Alejandro Cartagena
CL Desarrollos Gómez

El Camino Foodtruck answers to Monterrey's gastronomic needs. Combining Spanish and English, its name subtly communicates its transcultural flavours that extends to its typographic approach, expressing the truck's rough and Texan personality appealingly with reference to Americana and biker tattoo designs. The variety of writing style drawn up by hand highlights El Camino's artisanal cooking and its wide-ranging menu featuring burgers and vegetarian food.

ONE OF A KIND
Don't Try Studio

A visual exploration of slang terms for women, One of a Kind graphically interprets various common expressions in illustrations, pictures and mixed typography. Stripping any conceivable kind of offensive remarks, these images turn the focus back to the neutral qualities these words imply. Models dressed and posed as iconic pin-up girls and celebrities from the fifties suggest the tradition of using these slangs in daily language.

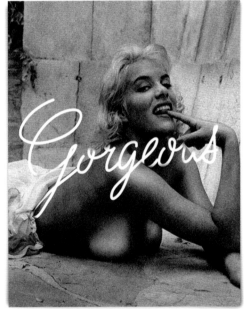

RIVADAVIA

Monotypo Studio

CL Cecilia de Quiroz

Put together as a fanciful platter of fresh and delicious food, branding for Italian-Argentinian restaurant RIVADAVIA draws inspirations from a diverse source. The logo with a cow suckling two men was a variant of Capitoline Wolf from Roman mythology, Romulus and Remus, but the system also features a fusion of food and related imagery that concoct a collective brand image united by detailed drawings.

LA FUSIÓN DEL

HORNO DE LEÑA

—*y el* ASADO ARGENTINO—

PIG'S PEARLS

Monotypo Studio

CL PIG´S PEARLS

Influences of Victorian age graphic style and 19th century English engravings prevail the visual identity of PIG's PEARLS, a gourmet burger restaurant in Guadalajara, Mexico. Fine drawings of a historic kitchen and a thoughtful brand approach immediately set the restaurant apart from other local fast food joints. The illustrations also hint at the use of fresh and premium ingredients that give the food its distinguishing flavours.

BIÈRES DU CHÂTEAU

A3 Studio

PH Michel Meier
CL Brasserie Artisanale du château Lausanne

Lausanne-based brewery Bières du château's beer are brewed in the most traditional way. For this reason A3 Studio has developed a graphic style which is both contemporary and traditional. The labels reference the sea world and are decorated with ropes. Where hand drawn illustrations emphasise the handmade production process inspired by old engravings and sailor tattoos, craft paper stresses the authenticity of the beer.

THE SUPERNATURAL

Inhouse Design

~~~~~~
CL And Co. Wines
~~~~~~

Playing on the wine's name, The Supernatural's bottle label was imagined as a cabinet of curiosities featuring taxidermy, apparatuses and otherworldly objects drawn from natural history. The idea continues on, with the beer's aroma references and the brewer's belief dancing across the label. A monochrome and metallic gold palette gives the beverage a tint of extra flavour.

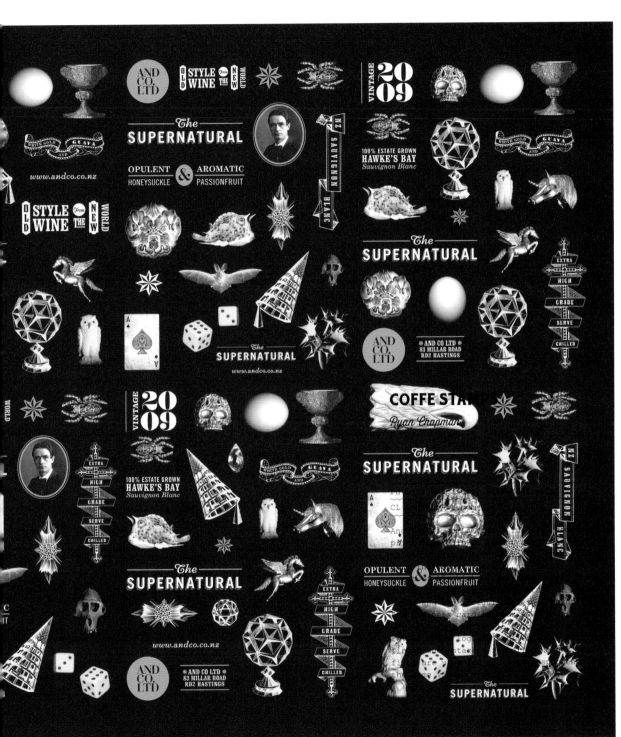

COFFE STAMPS
Ryan Chapman

THE SICILIAN

Bravo

The Sicilian serves revived Italian cuisine in New South Wales, Australia. Accompanying recipes from the 1940s is a brand system that references American gangster movie setting of the same era when food, money and family took priority. The theme runs seamlessly from dollar note-like vouchers to its tabloid-inspired breakfast menu, with TV fictional character Don Corleone making the headline. The typographic logo is crafted from the engraved inscriptions of firearms and the monogram of the shield, from an open gun chamber.

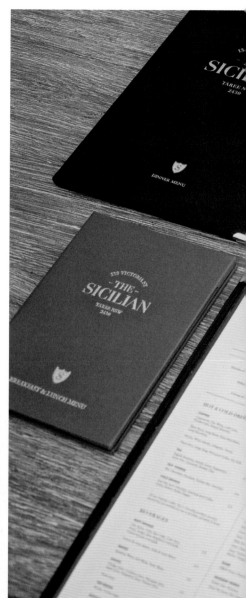

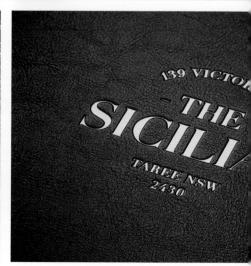

BAR GINGER

Power-nap Over

CL Bar Ginger

A logo and a customised logotype express medieval influences that subtly conforms with Bar Ginger's prohibition-style interior. Depicting a ladder leaning against a letter G, the sign invites the whisky bar's clientele to enter another side of the world for a pure journey of taste. A metallic and navy blue palette sets the mood for an unforgettable night out.

LUCHA LOCO

Bravo

CL Lucha Loco

With a moniker borrowed from the famous Mexican wrestler, Lucha Loco is a taqueria and bar that serves authentic Mexican street food in Singapore. Aiming for a rustic appearance as if the young bar has existed for decades, the restaurant's brand applications give way to a burst of Lucha Libra cultural cues, complimented by simple designed elements, such as a logo depicting a luchador performing an "Asai Moonsault". The business cards resembling vintage trading cards of wrestling celebs add a humorous touch.

HOTEL CYCLE

UMA/design farm

HOTEL CYCLE
HIROSHIMA ONOMICHI

IN SUPPOSE DESIGN OFFICE
PH Yoshiro Masuda
CL Discoverlink Setouchi Inc.

HOTEL CYCLE is part of Onomichi U2, a resort complex dedicated to cycling enthusiasts. The hotel's identity is characterised by a logotype and typesetting that run afloat on the walls, referencing the moment when guests were cycling leisurely around the many slopes in the city of Onomichi city, Hiroshima, Japan. Also an homage to the coastal city's shipbuilding and metalworking heritage, brass plays as an integral element in giving the identity a classic yet industrial look.

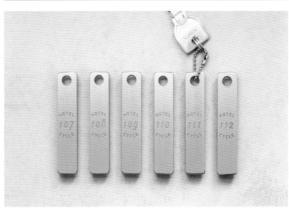

THE ASSEMBLY

Bravo

CL Benjamin Barker

The Assembly is a multi-label men's fashion store that also houses a café named The Assembly Ground. Targeting fun-loving and spontaneous gentlemen with an eye to quality, the shop's brand identity is a classic, versatile and playful one that contributes a nostalgic ambience in the retail space. Its logo, resembling the letter 'A' constructed with three sticks, reinforces the retail concept of combining the shop and café as a place of convocation.

SOPRA

Bravo

CL Sopra Cucina & Bar

Sopra Cucina & Bar is an Italian restaurant located at a corner of a busy shopping district in Jakarta. To put neighbouring night entertainment establishments in the shade, Bravo found inspiration in the razzle-dazzle of postwar Italian cinema and forged a glamorous identity for the restaurant. Realised as an illuminated grand signage and graphic logo, Sopra is an ode to the glamorous days when Hollywood, Federico Fellini films and Sophia Loren first captured their imaginations.

WOODLAND WINE MERCHANT

Perky Bros

CL Woodland Wine Merchant
PH Brett Warren

Woodland Wine Merchant is an eclectic wine
store in Nashville that carefully curates
wines from artisan producers who practice
natural and sustainable methods. It also
tirelessly hunts and gathers the best value
wines in the world. Inspired by this, the
team at Perky Bros designed a brand identity
that brings two worlds together: nature and
the unadorned 1960s qualities of the store's
premises. Besides positioning Tennessee's
red fox as the brand's symbol, they also
kept the typeface stark and utilitarian
with subtle quirks referencing gridless
mid-century layouts.

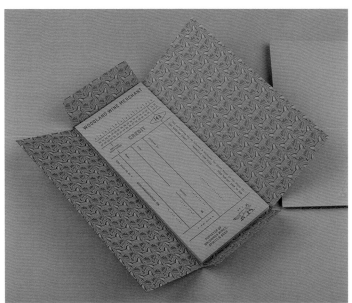

PASO CBD

Beach Design Studio

CL www.pasocbd.co.uk
PH Perry Graham
SC Ami Rogers

Paso is a prominent new player in the
growing CBD market, positioning itself as
'a cannabis brand for people who want to
take a step back and relax'. Drawing from
the nature of the products which contain
CBD - the laid-back, legal bit of cannabis
that aids relaxation and focus, the team at
Beach Design Studio created a top-to-bottom
visual identity that reflects a more open-
minded, balanced way of life using a calm
vintage-inspired mixture of illustrations,
typefaces, and colour.

PEDDLERS GIN CO

OMSE

PH Graeme Kennedy

CL Peddlers Gin Co

SC Family Type (Typeface Collaboration),
Render Studio & Rob Payne (3D Collaboration)

As China's first craft gin, Peddlers Gin Co carries the legacy of the secret societies that thrived in Shanghai, the world's biggest trading port during the early 20th century. Referencing the story and sign-writing style of the time, the team at OSME created a brand featuring a custom typeface and bottle design with a distinctive apothecary shape that takes inspiration from the city's peddlers of yesteryear. For the product launch, mahjong-related collateral and activation events were devised in line with the overall concept.

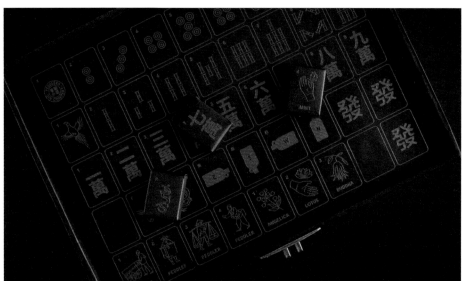

NOW SHOWING

Pengguin

CL Tai Kwun

'Now Showing' is a series of thematic movie
screenings presented by Tai Kwun, the former
Central Police Station compound-turned-art
and cultural hub in Hong Kong. In paying
tribute to the city's film culture of yore
when going to the cinema with loved ones
was considered a popular leisure activity,
Pengguin set out to design a visual identity
that recreates the distinct vibrant vibes
of old Hong Kong. The vintage Chinese
typography and decor elements serve to
transport viewers back to the good old days.

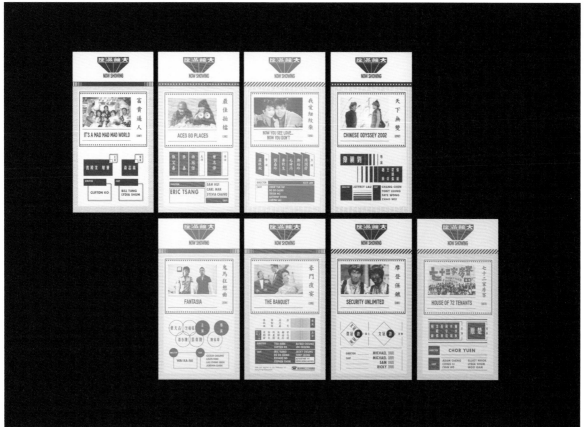

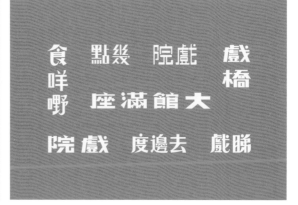

KOLKATA CHAI CO

Badal Patel

CL Kolkata Chai Co

Brothers Ayan and Ani Sanyal co-founded Kolkata Chai Co. (KCC) with the aim of extending the culture and heritage of its namesake to the streets of New York in an authentic and respectful way. To bring their vision to life, Badal Patel designed a striking visual identity that feels simultaneously nostalgic yet modern, featuring a clever combination of typefaces, vintage colours, and cheeky headlines. She also drew a chai-related mural that doubles as an educational tool and a fun photo opportunity inside the cafe.

KOLKATA CHAI CO

HOT CHAI	SMALL 8 OZ	LARGE 12 OZ
MASALA CHAI Assam black tea, organic whole milk, cardamom & fresh ginger	4	4.5
OATMILK MASALA CHAI Assam black tea, oatmilk, cardamom & fresh ginger	4.5	5
MA'S GINGER CHA black tea, ginger, cloves & jaggery	—	3.5
NIMBU CHAI black tea, spices & fresh lime	3.5 (4 OZ)	
KESAR CHAI chai topped with Spanish saffron	—	8
HALDI DOODH ginger, turmeric, honey & your choice of milk (+ ¢.50 for oatmilk)	4	4.5
AYURVEDIC TEA herbal blend of ashwagandha, valerian & local honey	3	3.5

HOT COFFEE	SMALL 8 OZ	LARGE 12 OZ
MODCUP COFFEE house drip blend, nutty, balanced	3	3.25
INDIAN FILTER COFFEE black coffee, scalded milk	4	4.5
CAFE DE OLLA black coffee, canela, piloncillo	—	4.25
CARDAMOM COFFEE black coffee, cardamom	—	4.25

COLD DRINKS	SMALL 12 OZ	LARGE 16 OZ
COLD BREW CHAI 18 hr immersion of black tea & spices	4	5
MASALA LIMCA fresh lime, spices	4.5	—

Add Ons

ROSE / CARDAMOM SYRUP	¢.25

SNACKS

BHEL PURI ~8
puffed rice, tamarind, micro greens

THAI BHEL PURI ~9
puffed rice, tamarind, fish sauce, lime

TOASTS*

MANGO ~11
AVOCADO
TOAST
sweet & tangy mango chutney

Naveen's
chaat toast ~10
chickpeas, cilantro, house-made masala

PANEER TOAST ~10
queso fresco, spice blend, greens

banana ~9
TOAST
topped with honey & cinnamon

GF BREAD +2

*SERVED ON BRIOCHE OR 5-GRAIN SOURDOUGH

APARTMENTARY

CFC

CFC were tasked to renew Apartmentary's corporate identity and restablish the lifestyle brand's remodelling service component by giving it a distinct yet cohesive voice in the process. Besides depicting the meaning of the brand name ('apartment' + 'documentary') itself, the studio also set out to express the basic characteristics of a remodelling service, which is to provide standardised beauty through the modularisation of construction. Derived from common visual motifs, the witty outcome delivers a sense of trustworthiness and a variety of experiences within one consistent system.

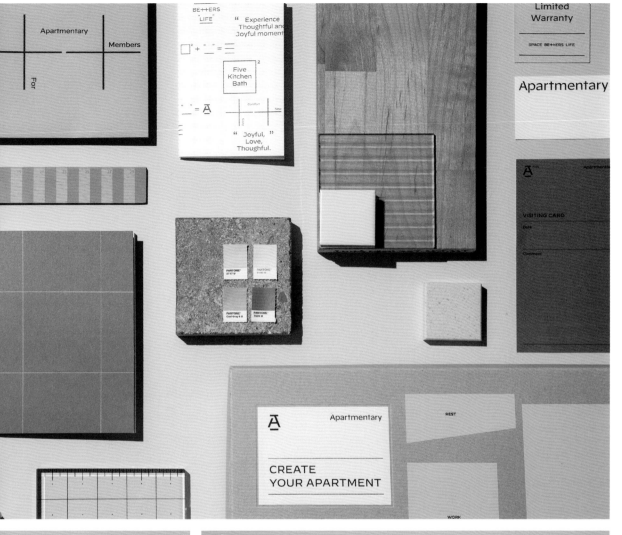

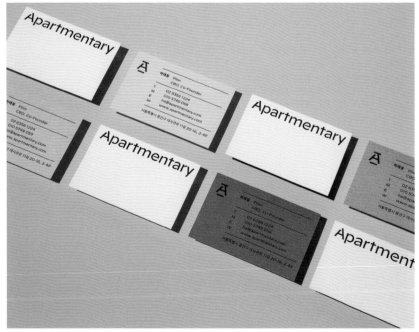

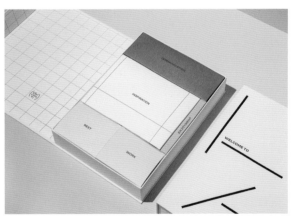

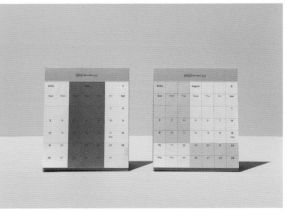

CUCA GREEN FONDA

Monotypo Studio

CL Daniela Alvarez, Javier Godinez, CUCA Founders
PH Eduardo Mejia Chávez

Cuca Green Fonda is an inn-type restaurant
that features organic and natural products in
Mercado Andares. In creating its visual identity,
Monotypo Studio were keen to not only reflect
strength and elegance, but also root the brand
in the traditional and spiritual aspects of
pre-Hispanic Mexican culture. Besides featuring
a 'curandera' or native healer holding two
branches of plants, the team also used hand-drawn
typographic elements that were inspired by the
first printing presses that opened in Mexico City
in the 16th century.

NAKAMA

Fundamental Studio

CL WOW music

Fundamental Studio believes that album packaging design can be a personal yet unique way for artistes or bands to connect with their listeners and share stories behind their albums' creation. For Hong Kong singer Endy Chow's 'Nakama' CD release, the studio designed a time machine of sorts by featuring a cassette tape-shaped photo album and a lyric book that references an old driving instruction manual. Every element from its packaging concept and structure to the paper selection and printing effects celebrates the distinct retro aesthetics of the 1980s.

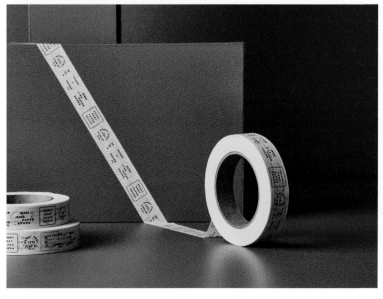

PENNY POST

SDCO Partners

CL Amy Rutherford

Penny Post is a sophisticated yet tongue-in-cheek boutique specialising in fine paper goods. The brand is inspired by 'the art of personal correspondence, the power of the written word, the smell of freshly printed things, the eclectic and the classic, the handmade, the everyday and once-in-a-lifetime celebrations'. In designing its visual identity, the SDCO Partners team looked to postage stamps from the past, combining them with a modern clean aesthetic from the present.

LA TEQUILA COCINA DE MÉXICO

Monotypo Studio

CL La Tequila Cocina de México

PH Diana Cristina Espinoza

For the brand identity of La Tequila Cocina de México, a restaurant specialising in Mexican gastronomy, the team at Monotypo Studio looked to the philosophy of the kitchen itself, which adds contemporary twists to traditional recipes. They also set out to represent the best of Mexico by connecting the past with the present, inspired by its roots and rich cultural heritage. The result is a beautiful fusion of old engravings, typography, and visual elements that serve to take diners on a journey of unique and unforgettable flavours.

PIPIRIS FRIES

Manifiesto

CL Pipiris Fries

Functioning as a 'dark kitchen' that specialises in food delivery without a traditional restaurant set-up, Pipiris Fries is one of the few places in Mexico City where customers can enjoy loaded chips/fries. In following the founders' wishes to create a brand that could capture the eccentric essence of their products, Manifiesto were tasked to design 'something that would make anyone drool just by reading the menu'. To build a unique universe around the brand, the team were inspired to go back in time – and stop it!

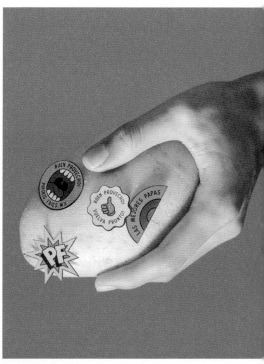

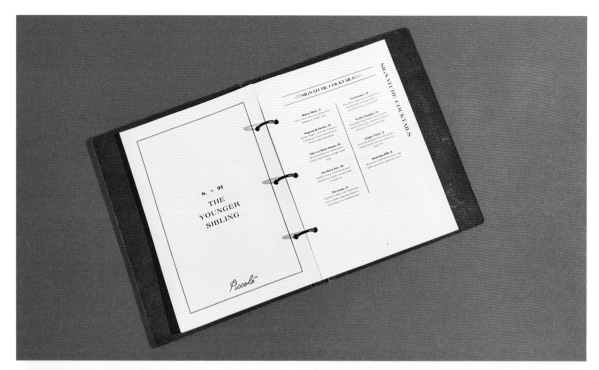

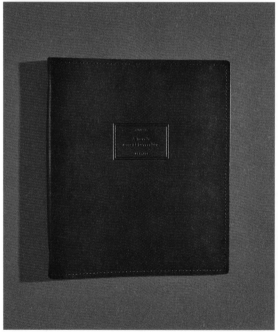

ARICCIA & PICCOLO

SDCO Partners

CL The Hotel Auburn University

SDCO Partners were tasked with reimagining the visual identity, story, and environment for Arricia & Piccolo, an authentic Italian trattoria and jazz lounge inside The Hotel at Auburn University. The team used custom letterforms to reflect the brand's roots and pay homage to vintage Italian design, pairing them with clean lines and soft corners for a contemporary touch. The logotype is reminiscent of speakeasy ephemera and music notes with modern lines that look inviting and approachable.

JOSÉ BARBA LIBRERO

TORO PINTO Studio

CL José Barba

For José Barba Librero, a bookstore in Guadalajara, TORO PINTO Studio worked with the client to create an accessible yet provocative brand with a retro-futuristic style. Inspired by the importance of books throughout history and 'Codex Seraphinianus, in which author-artist Luigi Serafini conceived an imaginary realm with its own rules, the team created a unique universe based on different illustrations depicting the process of knowledge being offered by books. They also developed an instruction chart to explain how our senses 'intervene' or work in this particular universe.

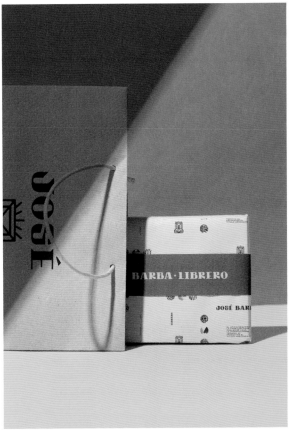

A3 Studio / Absoloot / Alana Louise / Anna Kövecses / artless Inc. / atelier bingo. / Badal Patel / Beach Design Studio / Bravo / Brian Steely / Bunker3022 / Bureau Rabensteiner / Ceci Peralta, José Velázquez / CFC / Claire Susie Jane / Colin Miller / Commando Group / David Cran / Diana Orozco / dn&co. / Dock 57 / Don't Try Studio / Duane Dalton / Estudi Àlex Ramon Mas / Estudio Yeyé / Facultative Works / Foreign Policy Design Group / Fundamental Studio / Futura / Geyser / Hey / HYPE Studio / Inhouse Design / innoise / Jared Bell / Joe Haddad / Judit Besze / Lo Siento / Mads Berg Illustration / Manifiesto / Milos Milovanovic / Monotypo Studio / Motoi Shito / Mucho / Non-Verbal Club / 0.00 Risograph Printing & Design ROOM / Oddds / OMSE / Onion Design Associates / Opus Nigrum / Pengguin / Perky Bros / Pol Pintó Fabregat / Power-nap Over / Ryan Chapman / Savvy Studio / Say What Studio / SDCO Partners / Studio Daad, Studio Turbo / studiowmw / Sunday Lounge / Table Six / The Good Folks Co. / Tobias Saul / Tom Grunwald / TORO PINTO Studio / Tseng Kuo-chan / UMA/design farm / vacaliebres / Violaine & Jérémy / Wang Zhi-Hong Studio / Wing's Art and Design Studio / Yondr Studio / Zdunkiewicz Studio / ZEALPLUS

A3 STUDIO

Consisting of graphic designer Yvo Hählen and visual communication designer Priscilla Balmer, A3 produces illustration, graphic design and typography with special attention to its prints quality, while also developing artistic productions. Founded in 2011 in Lausanne, Switzerland, A3 is regularly rewarded locally and abroad.

PAGES 140-141, 176-183, 233

ABSOLOOT

A creative studio providing premium print solutions, print consultation and management, Absoloot's passion is quality. They pay close attention to the details of every element of the print process, be it finding the best possible paper, ink or design. They work closely with designers, clients and businesses, combining traditional and innovative solutions to create timeless value and outstanding quality.

PAGES 148-149

ARTLESS INC.

Established in 2000 by Shun Kawakami, the interdisciplinary design and consulting firm works across all media including brand design, visual and corporate identity, advertising, packaging, product, video and motion graphics. The studio has won international awards including Cannes Gold Lions, NY ADC, D&AD and The London International Award.

PAGES 200-201

ATELIER BINGO.

The studio of Maxime Prou and Adèle Favreau who are both illustrators, surface pattern designers, and graphic designers from France. atelier bingo. loves to experiment with screenprinting and other graphic techniques to create colourful and abstract works.

PAGE 104

BEACH DESIGN STUDIO

Beach makes bold, disruptive and unconventional design solutions for brands, publications, people and beyond, working with clients it believes in to create brands that stand out.

PAGES 250-253

BELL, JARED

Bell is a Brooklyn-based musician and designer.

PAGES 122-123

BESZE, JUDIT

Currently living in Budapest, Hungary, Besze started three years ago as a freelance graphic designer. An autodidactic of graphic design, Besze's favourite creative field is food packaging design, besides working on branding projects for cafés, bakeries and restaurants.

PAGES 194-195

BRAVO

Bravo is a creatively-led design studio based in Singapore. Specialising in identity, brand development, printed communications and art direction, the independent workshop works with a variety of individuals and organisations to deliver thoughtful and engaging designs.

PAGES 156-159, 236-237, 240-241, 244-247

BUNKER3022

A branding and design studio based in Buenos Aires with a focus on the lifestyle and retail industry, Bunker3022 provides complete brand development from communication strategies, naming and consulting, photoshooting to brand promotion. They also work in the digital field on content generation and community management for social media.

PAGES 136-137

BUREAU RABENSTEINER

Bureau Rabensteiner is an Austrian design studio specialising in creative direction and graphic design. Since day one, Rabensteiner has always been about quality and detail.

PAGES 198-199

CFC

CFC is a Seoul-based multi-disciplinary design and photography studio that focuses on branding and packaging projects. It operates on the simple design principle that prioritises the understanding of content so that it can be transformed into its relevant form in the right context, creating new value and thoughtful experiences for businesses.

PAGES 260-263

CHAPMAN, RYAN

Chapman is a British illustrator who focuses on the simple use of soft shapes and minimal colours. He has collaborated on a range of projects with clients including Google, The New York Times, Microsoft, eBay and many others.

PAGES 100-101

CLAIRE SUSIE JANE

Claire Susie Jane is the studio of a young graphic designer from Strasbourg, France. A recent gratuate in Global Design and specialist in web design and branding, she has developed a real passion for editorial design. She adopts a global approach, allowing her to achieve a wide variety of projects.

PAGES 190-191

COMMANDO GROUP

Commando Group AS specialises in graphic design and illustration. They aim at merging their skills and knowledge into solutions that aid products and companies fighting to be visible and reach the target audience. Commando Group AS strongly believes that all design is strategic.

PAGES 184-185

CRAN, DAVID

Currently based between Vancouver and Seattle, Cran is a designer and illustrator with more than 30 years of experience and a passion for vintage-influenced typography, iconography and branding.

PAGES 026-029

DALTON, DUANE

A graduate of The Institute of Art, Design and Technology (IADT), Dalton is a graphic designer and artist from Dublin, Ireland. He is passionate about minimal and reductive design qualities that communicate a clear and precise message. This attribute is common throughout the majority of his work. Currently living and working in London, Dalton is now a designer at SEA Design.

PAGES 098-099

DN&CO.

dn&co. builds brands from the ground up covering print, digital, film and exhibition design. Strong strategic thinking as well as unapologetically modern aesthetics combined with a passion for space and architecture, has ensured that the team creates work that is original, appropriate and enduring.

PAGES 128-129

DOCK 57

Dock 57 are two freelance graphic designers from Russia, Sveta Shubina and Manar Shajri, who specialise in creating logotypes, corporate branding and illustrations. The duo have been creating visual identities of the highest quality according to the clients' needs since 2011.

PAGES 076-079

DON'T TRY STUDIO

Don't Try is a multidisciplinary studio based in Paris run by Quentin Monge, focusing on branding and illustration.

PAGES 228-229

ESTUDI ÀLEX RAMON MAS

The studio of Àlex Ramon Mas is based in Barcelona, specialising in graphic design, brand and corporate identity, illustration, advertising and web design. Always striving to understand and adapt to each client's specific needs, the studio combines strategy and design with attention to detail to create unique brand experiences in different media.

PAGES 010-021

ESTUDIO YEYÉ

Specialising in graphic design, photography, publicity and illustration, Estudio Yeyé's principal goal is to create relevant, innovative and work of the utmost quality that help clients' businesses grow.

PAGES 208-209

FACULTATIVE WORKS

Facultative Works was founded on the idea of working only with experimental and fascinating projects during the designers' free time for fun. After a while, the studio turned into a more significant operation while the main approach on work remained. The studio prefers the holistic approach to design by working in different fields such as illustration, identity, sound, editorial and furniture design.

PAGES 138-139

FOREIGN POLICY
DESIGN GROUP

Helmed by creative directors Yah-Leng Yu and Arthur Chin, Foreign Policy works on projects spanning creative/art direction and design, branding, brand strategy, digital strategy, strategic research and marketing campaigns for luxury fashion and lifestyle brands, FCMG, arts and cultural institutions and think tank consultancies.

PAGES 108-115, 144-147, 220-225

FUNDAMENTAL STUDIO

Based in Hong Kong, Fundamental believes that substantial communication is the key to creating and providing best designs and solutions to clients.

PAGES 154-155, 266-267

FUTURA

Futura is a design studio specialising in brand building. Founded by Iván García and Vicky González in 2008, the combination of two different sets of backgrounds and working methods has given the duo a unique way of approaching projects and finding balance between stiffness and rebellion.

PAGES 188-189

GEYSER

Gijs Dries or Geyser is a Belgium-based visual identity designer and brand builder with a focus on branding, typography and illustration. Fascinated by vintage signage and lettering, Dries is active in the vintage enthusiast community. Known for his minimal and straightforward designs with a retro touch, Dries gets inspiration by looking back in time.

PAGES 040-041

GRUNWALD, TOM

Tom Grunwald was born and raised in New York. He likes art, design, and going fast on two wheels.

PAGES 084-088

HADDAD, JOE

Haddad is a New York-based multidisciplinary designer. Besides taking a BFA in graphic design at the School of Visual Arts where he intends to graduate in 2017, Haddad is also currently an intern at GrandArmy. Prior to GrandArmy, he has worked at Mother New York and Deutsch Inc.

PAGES 130-131

HEY

Hey is a multidisciplinary design studio based in Barcelona, Spain. Specialising in brand management and editorial design, packaging and interactive design, Hey shares the profound conviction that good design means combining content, functionality, graphical expression and strategy.

PAGES 106-107

HYPE STUDIO

HYPE Studio is a small design studio based in Hanoi, Vietnam.

PAGES 192-193

INHOUSE DESIGN

Inhouse is an Auckland-based consultancy creating appropriate and effective solutions through simple, clear and well-crafted graphic design. Founded in 1995, it is a small practice often collaborating with other creative specialists, artists, architects, product designers and digital experts.

PAGES 196, 234-235

INNOISE

Founded by Jerry Luk in 2010, innoise specialises in branding, art direction, graphic and motion design besides a diverse collection of self-initiated artworks, projects and unique products. Luk believes that good design not only includes brilliant visuals, but also utilises a product's function and builds a distinctive image for a brand.

PAGES 186-187

KÖVECSES, ANNA

Kövecses is a Hungarian graphic designer living in the small seaside village of Cyprus, where she draws inspiration from magazine illustrations, book covers, fashion, and fine art. Her work is characterised by simple forms and bold colours, merging minimalism with a naive European nostalgia, which often includes alpine landscapes, mountain huts and friendly animals.

PAGES 102-103

LO SIENTO

Founded by Borja Martinez in 2005, Lo Siento is interested in taking over identity projects as a whole, covering the fields of corporative branding, packaging and editorial design. Their emphasis on materials results in solutions where graphic and industrial design go hand in hand. In 2014, Martinez was nominated to be part of the FAD assembly.

PAGES 126-127

LOUISE, ALANA

Half of The Good Folks Co., Louise was born with two hands and two first names.

PAGE 022

MADS BERG ILLUSTRATION

A graduate of the Danish Design School in 2001, Berg has been working independently as an illustrator while occasionally being a lecturer at design schools as well as an awards jury. Characterised by a style which translates classic poster art into a modern and timeless look, his work has won the Danish Design Prize and the 'Best Danish Children's Comic' prize.

PAGES 118-119

MANIFIESTO

Manifiesto is a design studio that specialises in branding and believes that ideas have the power to transform. As such, it transforms unique ideas into memorable concepts, images, spaces, and experiences as a way of giving something to the world – shaping the invisible.

PAGES 272-275

MILLER, COLIN

Half of The Good Folks Co., Miller is a keystoner and a huge Weakerthans fan.

PAGES 022-024

MILOVANOVIC, MILOS

Milovanovic is an award-winning graphic designer based in Serbia. His designs tend to lean on the illustrative side with a vintage, retro feel to it. The main focus of his craft is to reflect the essence, culture and personality of each client, creating interesting illustrative pieces that include logos, emblems, labels and packaging.

PAGES 034-039, 197

MONOTYPO STUDIO

Monotypo is a business service agency specialising in visual communication and graphic design. Their main objective is to leave a graphic impression of cleanliness, simplicity, aesthetics and functionality while satisfying clients' needs by in-depth analysis and tailor-made solutions.

PAGES 032-033, 080-083, 230-232, 264-265, 270-271

MUCHO

MUCHO specialises in art direction, strategic and corporate identities, editorial design, packaging, communications, digital design and motion graphics.

PAGES 204-205

NON-VERBAL CLUB

Formerly known as Atelier Martino & Jaña, Non-Verbal is a communication design studio based in Porto, Portugal. Obsessed with books, visual systems and typography, the team is vastly experienced in multidisciplinary design projects and have worked with notable clients such as Nike USA, NBC USA, European Capitals of Culture, The Vila Flor Cultural Centre, and Porto City Hall, among many others.

PAGES 105, 116-117, 210-211

O.OO RISOGRAPH PRINTING & DESIGN ROOM

The Taiwan-based studio is founded in 2014 by Pip Lu who graduated from Shih Chien University's Department of Communications Design. With an addiction to Risograph printing, Lu is also a visual artist of installation art and graphic design.

PAGES 132-135, 174-175

ODDDS

Founded in 2013 by designers based in Penang and Singapore respectively, Oddds focuses on graphic design, branding, photography, publication design, and illustration. Their work reflects significantly on behaviours, including how it draws attention and how it influences people. The team believes in aesthetics and futurism.

PAGES 090-091, 162-163

OMSE

OMSE is an independent design studio based in London. In creating meaningful brands that help businesses connect with their customers, its process is grounded in strategic and conceptual thinking, as the team believes that an effective brand is only built upon the platform of a compelling brand story - and that concept and craft demand equal consideration.

PAGES 254-255

ONION DESIGN ASSOCIATES

Onion Design Associates is a multidisciplinary graphic design studio co-founded by Andrew Wong in Taipei, Taiwan.

PAGES 212-213

OPUS NIGRUM

Opus Nigrum or Gabriel Oviedo currently works in an advertising agency as a senior graphic designer. It is his personal work that has achieved transcendence, with only him judging.

PAGES 052-057

OROZCO, DIANA

Orozco is a graphic designer and digital marketer with more than seven years of experience in logo design. Besides working with clients from the United States, Australia, Switzerland, the UK and Latin America, she is also the founder and director of HeyDesign Magazine.

PAGES 064-069

PATEL, BADAL

Badal Patel is a multi-disciplinary graphic designer whose diverse portfolio ranges from visual identity systems for mass consumer brands to niche new-to-world brands. Growing up as a first-generation Indian-American, Badal was immersed in two cultures at once, which is what she credits for her perspectives and constant need for chutney. Her aim is to add cultural relevance to the work she creates.

PAGES 258-259

PENGGUIN

Pengguin is a multi-disciplinary design studio in Hong Kong that focuses on visual communication, branding, editorial projects, spatial and exhibition design as well as motion and interactive design. It sets out to share different stories and concepts by triggering the chemistry between visual context and the media. The studio's work has been recognised and published internationally.

PAGES 256-257

PERALTA, CECI & VELÁZQUEZ, JOSÉ

Peralta and Velázquez attended design school together, became friends and from then on started working as a team. The duo developed most school projects together and realised a nice vibe going on. They went their separate ways upon graduation but still try working together on specific projects professionally.

PAGES 218-219

PERKY BROS

Perky Bros exists to help both startups and established brands gain clarity, value and distinction through design, visual identities, websites, packaging, print materials and any odd or end necessary for an authentic experience. The studio calls Nashville, Tennessee their home.

PAGES 202-203, 248-249

PINTÓ FABREGAT, POL

A former student at Eina University who has worked with Esiete, PFP disseny graphic, Pol is currently working with Dani Rubio Arauna on corporate identities, communication strategy, editorial design, exhibitions, and signage projects.

PAGES 124-125, 170-173

POWER-NAP OVER

Founded in Hong Kong by Vita Mak in 2013, the studio works across a diverse range of projects including art direction, branding, editorial, event, packaging and website design. At the same time, the team also develops products and independent publications. They intend to use products, graphics and text to express opinions about living.

PAGES 238-239

SAUL, TOBIAS

Saul is a lettering artist and graphic designer from Düsseldorf, Germany. Starting with graffiti and illustration at an early age, his passion for letters and layouts continued while he studied communication design with a focus on logo, branding and packaging. All of his work begins with pen and paper, digitalised later for finishing touches.

PAGES 060-063

SAVVY STUDIO

A multidisciplinary studio dedicated to developing brand experiences that generate emotions between clients and target audiences, Savvy Studio is composed of specialists in marketing, communication, graphic design, industrial design, creative copywriting and architecture. The studio also collaborates with talented artists and designers worldwide.

PAGES 226-227

SAY WHAT STUDIO

Say What Studio is a graphic design studio based in Paris run by Benoit Berger and Nathalie Kapagiannidi. Bound by a common passion, the pair founded the studio after graduating from the ECV school in 2011.

PAGES 050-051

SDCO PARTNERS

SDCO Partners are a multi-disciplinary team of designers, developers, storytellers, illustrators, thinkers, and strategists designing thoughtful, non-traditional, and holistic solutions that breathe life into new, evolving, and storied brands.

PAGES 268-269, 276-277

SHITO, MOTOI

Shito is an art director and graphic designer based in Tokyo, Japan.

PAGES 120-121

STEELY, BRIAN

Steely is an American designer widely known for his unique line logos. His work reinforces that it is not only the graphics that begin unravelling what a company does, but also the style it was created in. Using simple line-art, he manages to produce a range of diverse and inspiring logo designs for a number of outlets. From food products to bike head badges, his style works for every single one.

PAGES 070-075

STUDIO DAAD & STUDIO TURBO

Studio Daad and Studio Turbo are both typography-based design studios from the Netherlands. The work of Studio Daad mostly represents itself as handcrafted designs, while the work of Studio Turbo is mostly digitally created.

PAGES 142-143

STUDIOWMW

A design agency based in Hong Kong with footsteps in the global marketplace, studiowmw was founded by Sunny Wong. Specialising in brand building, its work comprises identity and environmental design, packaging and product design, website and physical store design, as well as commerce and charity work. studiowmw believes that mutual trust and relationships are the key to successful brands.

PAGES 150-153

SUNDAY LOUNGE

Sunday Lounge is the studio of Jared Jacob who lives and works in Salida, Colorado, USA.

PAGES 042-049

TABLE SIX

Table Six is an agile graphic design studio from Jakarta, Indonesia. Their versatile characteristic as a team of creatives, leads them to interesting clients from different industries. They indulge themselves in doing what they love, and love to collaborate with passionate people who believe in their products or services.

PAGES 164-167

THE GOOD FOLKS CO.

The Good Folks are Colin Miller and Alana Louise who claim themselves to be five foot small and six foot tall.

PAGE 025

TORO PINTO STUDIO

TORO PINTO is a specialised research cluster open to creative experimentation. The studio is constantly finding new ways to understand culture as a means to develop brands that express strong and expandable visual and written narratives.

PAGES 278-279

TSENG, KUO-CHAN

Tseng is a Taiwanese graphic designer who was born in 1990 in Tainan. A graduate in visual communication design from National Yunlin University of Science and Technology, Tseng is working as a freelancer, specialising in graphic design, visual identity and branding, publications, book covers, posters, commercial photography, and film-making.

PAGE 089

UMA/DESIGN FARM

Founded by art director and designer Yuma Harada in 2007, UMA/design farm works to provide book design, graphic design, exhibition design, space design, and art direction.

PAGES 168-169, 242-243

VACALIEBRES

vacaliebres is Alberto Vacca Lepri, who was born in Genoa, Italy in 1985. A graduate of the Fine Arts Academy in Urbino in 2011, vacaliebres has been freelancing with two agencies in Milan and New York.

PAGES 092-095

VIOLAINE & JÉRÉMY

An illustration and graphic design studio based in Paris, Violaine Orsoni and Jérémy Schneider are a team of artistic directors, graphic designers and illustrators. Their projects vary from fabric pattern design to magazine design and brand identities. Their clients include Dior, le Coq Sportif, the National Orchestra of Lorraine, Influencia Magazine, Tiffany and Co. and music labels like Ekler'o'shock.

PAGES 216-217

WANG ZHI-HONG STUDIO

Wang was born in 1975 in Taipei and started his studio in 2000. The six-time winner of Golden Butterfly Awards, Taiwan's highest honour for excellence in book design, has also received international recognitions, including Kaoru Kasai's Choice Award and Excellent Works from Tokyo Type Directors Club Annual Awards.

PAGES 214-215

WING'S ART AND DESIGN STUDIO

Wingsart.net is a collection of ready-made illustrations and design resources by freelance illustrator and graphic designer Christopher Wing King. With nearly two decades of experience, Wing has worked with clients ranging from restaurants, and toy companies to blues bands and burlesque troupes.

PAGES 030-031

YONDR STUDIO

The studio of Nathan Yoder, who is
an illustrator and designer from
Tulsa, Oklahoma. Currently located
in Seattle, Washington, he specialises in pen and ink illustration as
well as hand lettering and branding.

PAGES 206-207

ZDUNKIEWICZ STUDIO

A small studio based in Warsaw, Po-
land founded by graphic designer
Krzysztof Zdunkiewicz. Focusing on
branding and print projects while
also working on interactive, app and
web projects, Zdunkiewicz is an art
director with seven years of experience in advertising and branding.
He loves simple and clean ideas, and
is obsessed with vintage and black
and white projects.

PAGES 058-059

ZEALPLUS

ZEALPLUS is a design studio based
in Osaka, Japan. Founded in 2005,
the studio specialises in communication design, graphic design and
web design.

PAGES 160-161

ACKNOWLEDGEMENTS

WE WOULD LIKE TO THANK ALL THE DESIGNERS, STUDIOS, AND COMPANIES WHO WERE INVOLVED IN THE PRODUCTION OF THIS BOOK FOR THEIR SIGNIFICANT CONTRIBUTION TO ITS COMPILATION. WE WOULD ALSO LIKE TO EXPRESS OUR GRATITUDE TO ALL THE PRODUCERS INVOLVED FOR THEIR INVALUABLE OPINIONS AND ASSISTANCE, AS WELL AS THE PROFESSIONALS IN THE CREATIVE INDUSTRY WHO WERE GENEROUS WITH THEIR INSIGHTS AND FEEDBACK THROUGHOUT THE ENTIRE PRODUCTION PROCESS. LAST BUT NOT LEAST, TO THOSE WHO MADE SPECIFIC INPUT BEHIND THE SCENES BUT WERE NOT CREDITED IN THIS BOOK, WE ACKNOWLEDGE AND APPRECIATE ALL YOUR EFFORT AND CONTINUOUS SUPPORT.

FUTURE EDITIONS

IF YOU WISH TO PARTICIPATE IN VICTION:ARY'S FUTURE PROJECTS AND PUBLICATIONS, PLEASE SEND YOUR WEBSITE OR PORTFOLIO TO

SUBMIT@VICTIONARY.COM